Bible Study Workbook

A Beginner-Friendly Guide to Unlocking the Essentials of All 66 Books

Table of Contents

Introduction

The Bible can seem intimidating when first approaching it; staring at that thick book on the shelf gathering dust could be a little demotivating. Then you open it and find complicated English written in dense paragraphs, and after a few sentences, you get completely discouraged.

The scriptures do not have to be viewed like this complex work reserved only for the world's top scholars. With keys to understanding the text and themes running through the 66 books of the Bible, you will be seamlessly guided through the study process. As a historical and spiritual text, navigating each book's multiple layers can be a fulfilling task that reveals much about yourself. As you go through the details of each book, an overarching narrative of hope and redemption emerges as the sovereignty of God is unveiled.

Studying the Bible should not purely be an intellectual exercise. As you dive through its pages, the divine messages come alive, and your heart is realigned with worshipping God. Believers and non-believers alike can benefit from this workbook as it encourages you to grasp the Biblical text through a scholarly lens using the many lessons in its pages as a pathway to connect with the Most High. This way, a transformation into a better version of yourself is facilitated.

The workbook's theoretical aspects uncover theological, political, linguistic, and ethical meanings. The practical exercise helps you apply the text to your life in a meaningful way. Some Bible workbooks are too focused on education, while others do not provide the context to make spiritual wisdom come alive. This workbook perfectly balances the scholarly and spiritual to create a comprehensive guide that dissects every corner of the scriptures.

From the Mosaic Law and the wisdom teachings of Psalms and Proverbs to the prophetic writings and the saving grace of the Gospels, you walk along the path of a living ancient tradition. By exploring this timeless wisdom, you are reintroduced to the spiritual side of your being, awakening the reality of the God of Israel as described in the Bible.

Trace the steps of the prophets to the apostles as the covenantal system climaxes in the coming of Jesus, who died for the sins of the world. Discover the details and context of the Gospels and learn why they are still relevant in the modern world. Furthermore, unpack the intricacies of prophecy so that you can grasp the mysteries of symbolic writing and fully embrace the messages applicable today. By working diligently through the theories and activities on these pages, you will gain knowledge or a foundation to understand and embody the scripture's teachings.

Section 1: Understanding the Bible's Historical Context

The Bible is not a historical book; it is more of a *spiritual text*. However, there are historical aspects of the scriptures you must grasp to understand the book fully. Studying history can get complicated because it is not a hard science, like engineering or physics, where proof and evidence are more solid and practical.

Most history is based on archeological evidence and testimonies interpreted through various lenses. Moreover, those who wrote the texts using historical evidence also had their own views and biases. Therefore, the study in this field is robust, but many scholars disagree. This book provides the historical context of the Bible from different viewpoints to give you a complete and unbiased picture of the text. In this way, you can put the puzzle together and critically draw your own conclusions based on the available data.

The Bible is not a historical book because it is more of a spiritual text.
*NYC Wanderer (Kevin Eng), CC BY-SA 2.0 <https://creativecommons.org/licenses/by-sa/2.0>,
via Wikimedia Commons:
https://commons.wikimedia.org/wiki/File:Gutenberg_Bible,_Lenox_Copy,_New_York_Public_L
ibrary,_2009._Pic_01.jpg*

Exploring the Bible starts by understanding that it is not only one holy book but a compilation of 66 books, depending on the canon you are looking into. For example, the Ethiopian Orthodox canon contains 81 books, significantly more than the widely accepted King James Version. Through various historical concepts and geopolitical occurrences, understanding of the Bible has shifted so it gets read differently, depending on theological schools or scholarly interpretations. Therefore, the text is living and evolving according to time and region. Sifting through these complex dynamics requires a lifetime of study. However, a snapshot can point you in the right direction to facilitate more informed opinions.

The History of the Bible

The history of the Old Testament is the establishment of an Israelite identity. The Bible will, of course, be understood differently by different readers based on the preexisting beliefs and opinions of the reader. The more literalist strain of Biblical interpretation accepts that the Exodus account of Israel becoming a nation in Egypt and the lineage of Israelites coming from Abraham is true. However, when the archeological evidence is weighed up, this narrative has problems.

The Israelite nation and its beliefs were likely an amalgamation of people who emerged from the ancient Near East. They were put in a position politically and culturally to separate themselves to establish a new nation. Clues to this view are hidden in the text, namely through the formation of the law. In Deuteronomy, there are laws like not planting different seeds on one section of land, prohibiting wearing mixed fabrics, and forbidding intermarriage with foreigners. These laws were intended to emphasize separation and solidify the establishment of a new nation from the plurality of the Western Semites.

Essentially, the Israelites are the Canaanites, although the Bible sets it up as a narrative of conquer. The Israelite identity is a continuation of Canaanite traditions that were repackaged into the chosen people's narrative. For example, the name Yahweh comes from the Canaanite pantheon, and El, a general term referring to deities, can be tied to a god with the same name. Therefore, when the Bible is studied historically, and the aspect of divine revelation is minimized, you'll find that the overarching story is completely transformed. Instead of the Canaanites or Western Semites being framed as villainous, they are the progenitors of the Israelite culture.

When you get to the New Testament, another evolution of the Israelite identity emerges. The best way to think about the New Testament doctrines is open-sourcing of the Israelite faith. No longer is the inheritance of the Kingdom of God focused on birthright, but now readers are introduced to the concept of adoption into the Kingdom through Jesus Christ's sacrifice. This open-sourced approach to religion radically shifted the tribal and nationalistic ties of how faith was understood for centuries. Now, Gentiles were also allowed into the Kingdom through adoption. Where Israel was once thought of as the son of God, the Christian framework now places Jesus in that position, creating salvation through Christ as the truth.

Biblical Timelines

History continuously evolves, and because the Bible is a living tradition, the story has not yet completely unfolded. Even though the Bible was canonized by the third century, understanding of the text is continuously changing. Religious movements like the protestant reformation, later developments in the New World, and today, where texts are constantly interpreted through contemporary lenses, means the story is continuously evolving. Therefore, you need to think of Biblical history as alive and dynamic.

However, if the focus is placed on the writing, compiling, and canonizing of the Bible, then the historical timeline can be divided into seven key periods.

Late Bronze Age

This era of Bible tradition development can be considered as the age when the foundations of religion and traditions were laid. The Late Bronze Age spanned between 1550 BC and 1200 BC. The Ugarit – in northern Syria – was a bustling cosmopolitan city where many diverse religious and cultural practices were embraced, some of which evolved into Israelite customs and law. Deities such as Asherah, Baal, and El were worshiped in that region. All three are mentioned by name in the Bible, and one of them, El or Elohim, references the God of the Israelites.

During Pharoah Merneptah's reign, Israel is mentioned in the Merneptah stela (an inscription by Merneptah, a pharaoh in ancient Egypt who reigned from 1213 to 1203 BCE), which ties to the Exodus narrative of Israelite slaves in Egypt. The stela boasts victories over various Canaanite groups, including Israel, ending with the statement, "Everyone who is restless, he has been bound." It is still arguable that the Biblical Exodus under the prophet Moses was a literal event because of a lack of archeological evidence of millions of people camping in the Sinai desert. However, the Exodus account may have been a true but exaggerated occurrence.

Iron I Period

The first Iron Age was when the Israelite identity had been firmly crafted, and you can begin to see texts emerging. Some sayings in Genesis and poems in Judges 5 originate from this period. This era of the Israelite nation was predynastic, with loosely cooperating tribes claiming Israelite identity. Archeology from this period discovered inscriptions on metal items like arrowheads, including names and burial verses. Near the end of the Iron Age I, Israel got its first king, Saul, who would precede the famous and legendary King David.

Iron II Period

This period in Israelite history is when the nation emerged as a powerful force in the region. The rule of King David and his treaty with Tyre established Israel as a hegemony over neighboring cultures. Following King David, the famous King Solomon established trade and diplomatic relations with Egypt, and the Jerusalem temple was built.

When King Solomon died, Israel was thrown into turmoil, resulting in a split into the Northern Kingdom of Israel and the Southern Kingdom of Judah. Jeroboam I became the first king in the North. The Gezer calendar inscription was created between 900 BC and 800 BC, one of the earliest sources of written Hebrew. Sections of Psalms and portions of 2 Samuel may trace the origins back to this period. It is theorized that parts of the Old Testament come from the compilation of two source texts: the J source (which uses the name *Yahweh* and was later translated into Jehovah) and the E source (using the name *El* or *Elohim*). The J source may have originated from the Southern Kingdom around 900 to 800 BC.

Between 882 and 871 BC, Omri established the capital of the Northern Kingdom in Samaria. Later, King Ahab created a coalition with Tyre, which was solidified by his marriage to the infamous Jezebel. During this time, many of the Bible's most prominent prophets emerged, such as Elijah, Elisha, Isaiah, and Hosea. In the second Iron Age, the bulk of Deuteronomy was written. Hoshea, the last king of Israel, acted as a vassal for the Assyrian Empire. Many Old Testament writings were likely circulating in the Second Iron Age, including the Psalms, Proverbs, and First and Second Kings. The Israelites entered the Babylonian captivity with the fall of Jerusalem and the destruction of the temple.

Persian Period

In this period, Judah became a province of the Persian Empire. Under the rule of Cyrus, the Israelites were allowed to return to their homeland. An initial group of Judaens, led by the governor Sheshbazzar, returned to Judah. The next governor of the Persian province of Judah was Zerubbabel. He rebuilt the Temple of Jerusalem, but it was not as prestigious as the first. In collaboration with the religious leader Jeshua, under the inspiration of the prophecy of Haggai, they undertook this project to restore the dignity of Israel. Following the reconstruction of the temple, Nehemiah rebuilt the walls of Jerusalem. The books of Daniel, Esther, Chronicles, Song of Songs, and the priestly compilation of Psalms were completed between 300 BC and 400 BC. You also find that Job, in its modern form, may have been completed at this time.

Hellenistic Period

The Hellenistic Period of Biblical history spans from 333 BC to 165 BC, beginning when Alexander the Great conquered Egypt and the Levant. The establishment of the Samaritan priestly order began due to conflicts within the priesthood. Once Alexander died, his kingdom was split between his generals, including Ptolemaic Egypt and the Seleucids in Syria. By the mid-200s, the earliest Dead Sea Scrolls were written, and the Greek Septuagint translation of the Bible was written. Judea revolted against the Seleucids, who ushered in the Maccabean monarchy. By the end of the Hellenistic period, many Old Testament scriptures were distributed widely, and the Torah and the prophetic writings were considered authoritative.

Maccabean Monarchy

The Maccabean monarchy started with the defeat of the Seleucids, who had dedicated the temple in Jerusalem to Zeus. Once their armies were defeated, the temple was restored, instituting Judas Maccabeus's rule over Judea. The restoration of the temple is celebrated in the book 1 Maccabees. Following the rule of Judas, his brother Johnathon took over and fought the Nabateans, prompting the fortification of Jerusalem. In this era, conflicts within the priesthood resulted in the development of multiple communities, one of which was the Dead Sea Scroll Movement.

Roman Period

This is probably the most popular period in the mainstream consciousness because it was the era in which Jesus Christ was born. Since Christianity is the most practiced faith in the world today, it makes sense that this era would be primarily focused on it. The Roman period significantly impacted the modern Jewish religion because this was when the Talmudic writings were completed. The New Testament books were compiled around the years 50 to 100 AD based on oral traditions passed around by the growing Christian religion. In 70 AD, the Romans destroyed the Jerusalem temple. Eventually, the Romans embraced Christianity as the state religion after years of persecuting the Christians, which helped spread the faith to become as widely practiced as it is today.

Timeline Activity

In the space below, draw a timeline of the key periods of Biblical History. Highlight important events and explain how they link to what is contained in the Bible narrative.

Geopolitics and the Israelite Identity

Many tribes inhabited the ancient Near East, which resulted in a plurality of spiritual beliefs. As it was a trade route, nomadic tribes would cross the area, contributing to the local systems. Adding to this mixing pot, conquest and conflict within the Near East fundamentally shaped how religion would be understood. Examining the Biblical text, you find influences from these various groups. For example, the New Testament was written predominantly in Greek due to the Hellenistic contribution to Judaic culture at the time.

Exploration of the Bible requires knowing that it occurred in different areas and times throughout the Middle East. The influence of Assyrians, Egyptians, Hittites, and Edomites is clear when the text is understood as having emerged in a particular context. Some even cite ancient Egypt as influencing the Bible through resurrection narratives and rising gods and as one of the earliest forms of monotheism under the Akhenaten rule. However, instead of one culture feeding into another, a more accurate view would be that the intermixing in the area facilitated the emergence and spreading of similar ideas. For example, the Persian Zoroastrianism religion may have influenced Jewish ideas of an adversarial force personified as Satan and the positive of God existing in a battle.

Within the Israelite traditions, there was a diversity of thought. Part of the reason that the Jewish religious establishment was against the emergence of Jesus as a Messianic figure was the disastrous impacts similar thoughts had had in the past. Jewish opinions at the time were split between two major schools: the teachers who focused on the law and the messianic schools that prophesied a coming messiah that would free them from Roman rule. Jesus was not the first or only messianic figure to emerge in rebellion against the Romans. More violent messiah prototypes who led rebellions and the masses of people who followed them were quickly dealt with and killed by Roman soldiers. The priestly and leadership class of Judah noticed this repeating cycle, so the establishment pushed to move away from apocalyptic interpretations of texts for self-preservation. Hence, they may have had problems with Jesus, one in a long line of Messiahs taking on this archetype.

Through the window of understanding internal Jewish conflicts, disagreements between tribes inhabiting the same area, and the numerous conflicts that occurred, many of the Bible's laws, teachings, and interpretations begin to make sense. Besides the geopolitics of literature, there is also the element of divine revelation that deals with fulfilled prophecy and the supernatural realm. Many scholars refrain from this supernatural aspect of the Bible because there is no way to prove or study it. However, if you consider divine revelation to be true, it can reframe the meaning of the Bible and further contribute to the book's geopolitical formation because the decisions of believers are generally driven by their faith and how they interpret their beliefs. The strong belief of martyrs who died for Christianity in its earliest days is why it spread so far. People were in awe of the conviction early believers demonstrated, so they were enticed to join the faith that believers were willing to die for. Therefore, the interplay between faith, politics, and history makes the Bible one of the most captivating textual compilations to ever exist.

The Bible and Critical Thinking

Christianity, Judaism, and the modern understanding of the Bible could have looked entirely different had a few key moments panned out differently. Therefore, critical thinking in the Biblical sense requires minimizing biases and reviewing all the information available in order to draw conclusions about the text. Studying the Bible takes a lifetime of dedication. There are numerous translations and theological understandings of the text, so you will find many Christian denominations and Jewish schools of thought with conflicting ideas, even though leaders have dedicated innumerable hours to seeking the truth of the Bible.

New ways of interpreting the text are emerging with movements like progressive Christianity that highlight the social justice aspects of the Gospel and aim to make Christianity more inclusive for various groups like the LGBT community. In the modern age, much information is emerging, and data travels so quickly that you can reach it immediately. Moreover, you have more access to information than many of the Biblical scholars and enthusiasts of the past would have had. It means that critical thinking is more important now than ever because of the influx of information and the flood of conflicting views.

The crux of critical thinking is adjusting to new information instead of remaining firm and immovable.

The crux of critical thinking is adjusting to new information instead of remaining firm and immovable. Being open-minded to new information and analyzing it according to the latest research gives you the foundational principle to a fuller understanding of the Bible. Considering factors like translations, politics, history, and the theological interpretation of the text gives you a well-rounded view. With open-minded study, you can inch closer to a complete view of this ancient compilation of books that have so profoundly shaped the world.

As you continue through these chapters, you will gain more information about the Bible and be taught to think critically and question the narratives placed before you so that you can assess the details with a fine-toothed comb and unearth the hidden gems.

How do you currently understand the Bible?

_____
_____
_____
_____
_____

What influenced that view?

_____

_____

_____

_____

_____

Are you open to having those views challenged? Why, or why not?

_____

_____

_____

_____

_____

Research Activity

Research the differences that emerge when a person accepts divine revelation to interpret the Biblical text and when a person rejects supernatural interventions.

How can you understand the development of the ancient Israelite religion and later Christianity through the interpretation of divine revelation?

How can you understand the development of the Israelite religion and Christianity if divine revelation is rejected?

What are the possible geopolitical and historical reasons that the Torah, or Pentateuch, was written and compiled as it is known in modern times?

What geopolitical and historical reasons resulted in the transition from the oral traditions of the early followers of Christ to seeing the Gospels codified into standardized scripture?

Section 2: Genesis to Deuteronomy: The First 5 Books

The Bible's first five books, the Torah or the Pentateuch, are foundational to the text's narrative structure. The beauty of scripture is that it has been written from different authors' viewpoints in varying cultural contexts over hundreds of years, yet an overarching narrative has emerged. The structures and moral lessons of the Bible's first five books continue to echo and unfold as the story progresses.

The Bible's first five books, the Torah or the Pentateuch, are foundational to the text's narrative structure.

In this Chapter, you will dive into the thematic elements of the Torah and examine how you can apply these lessons today. From the formation of modern law and how civilization is shaped by personal experiences, the Torah is an incredible mirror to hold up in order to reflect on your life and society. The Pentateuch is arguably the most essential part of the Bible because the stories that follow are built onto the themes already revealed through its powerful narratives. You explore God's relationship with humankind and, by extension, their interactions with each other to reveal miraculous stories of judgment, mercy, redemption, and salvation from Genesis to Deuteronomy. The timeless stories and principles they reveal are still as relevant as they ever were, so their exploration can unpack a lot about yourself and how your life can embody some of the highest principles of truth.

Plotting Key Narratives from Genesis to Deuteronomy

The central plot that runs through the Bible's first five books, or the Torah, the Hebrew word for law, is God's tumultuous relationship with mankind. The Israelite God is a radical reframing of how the ancient world understood deities. Although many of the same practices and agreements were required by the God of the Bible and other gods, the central difference is love. The vital focal point in the Torah is that although God gets angry and curses His people, a fatherly relationship is maintained throughout the constant struggle between obedience and rebellion.

Genesis

The word *Genesis* can be translated as the beginning. Genesis focuses on the start of the cosmos and sets the stage for the beginning of God's relationship with humankind. The cosmos begins as this chaotic and inhabitable place, or as the Bible calls it, "formless and void." Then God orders it, creating a world that He constantly refers to as "good." The Bible introduces the first humans, Adam and Eve. Some interpret them as literal people, while others take the story more symbolically. Either way, there is meaning embedded into their names. Adam means "Humanity," and Eve means "Life." In this way, these two characters were the first representatives of what humanity's relationship with God would look like.

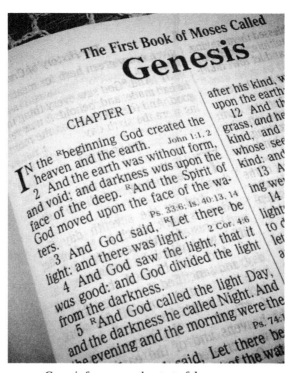

Genesis focuses on the start of the cosmos.
John Snyder, CC BY-SA 3.0 <https://creativecommons.org/licenses/by-sa/3.0>, via Wikimedia Commons https://commons.wikimedia.org/wiki/File:The_Book_of_Genesis.jpg

Adam and Eve had not yet received the law, which would come later with the prophet Moses. However, they were given a rule not to eat the fruit from the Tree of Knowledge of Good and Evil. When they ate the fruit, it represented a departure from following the desires of God to humanity relying on their understanding, which inevitably came with devastating consequences.

The theme of humans following their desires against what God has asked them to do is repeated throughout the Torah, especially in the first Book of Genesis. You get the first murder where Cain killed Abel. Then Lamech, his descendent, brags that his wickedness is even greater, eventually leading to the tower of Babel, where humanity attempts to build a structure to reach the heavens. Now, the theme of humankind following their whims gets fleshed out a little more because, instead of following God's guidelines to get closer to Him on His terms, they attempted to achieve it through their own struggles. God knows this will not end well because impure humans cannot get close to Him without dying, so He shows them mercy by confusing their languages and splitting them into nations. Each nation has its god at this time, but through His relationship with Abraham, the God of Israel reveals that he is greater than them, which will become more significant later in the narrative in Exodus.

Before Abraham, you get Noah, who built the ark before God flooded the Earth. After generations of wickedness, God finally got fed up and decided to end the world. Noah and his family members enter the ark as the world is flooded. This is one of the most striking depictions of God's justice and mercy because He does not destroy everyone but gives a few faithful individuals a chance. The next major player in the Biblical narrative was Abraham, through whom God established the covenantal system. God made three major promises to Abraham. First, he would have many descendants. Secondly, he would get land for his people and, lastly, all nations would be blessed through his seed.

An interpretation of Noah's ark.

Abraham's son Jacob received his birthright, and he had twelve sons. His favorite son was Joseph. Jacob gave Joseph a colorful coat, which made his brothers jealous. They plotted to murder him but ended up selling him into slavery. With the gifts God gave Joseph, he rose through the ranks and became one of Egypt's most powerful people. Famine struck many nations in the Middle East, which led Joseph's brothers to seek refuge in Egypt. They arrived in Egypt to find their brother held a high position and could help them. He remarked on how their plans for wickedness, God, had turned into plans for prosperity. This was the instant when the transmutation aspect of the Torah, and by extension, the Bible, was initially revealed because God's all-knowing might could transform evil into righteousness even when it seemed hopeless.

Exodus

Some generations after Joseph, the Israelites were enslaved in Egypt by a wicked pharaoh. The Exodus narrative of God delivering the Israelites out of captivity under the leadership of Moses began. Pharoah refused to free the Israelites, which brought plagues to Egypt. Through these terrifying plagues, justice was emphasized. For example, the final plague was killing the Egyptians' firstborn sons, just like the pharaoh commanded the murder of the eldest sons of Israel. The Israelites had to slaughter a Passover lamb and rub the blood on their doors to avoid their firstborns being killed. Blood in the Bible represents life, so this symbolizes that only life could enter the doors of the Israelites. This is linked to the later part of the Torah (in Deuteronomy), when Moses urged the Israelites to choose life.

The Exodus provides the narrative of God delivering the Israelites out of captivity.
Distant Shores Media/Sweet Publishing, CC BY-SA 3.0
<https://creativecommons.org/licenses/by-sa/3.0>, via Wikimedia Commons
https://commons.wikimedia.org/wiki/File:Book_of_Exodus_Chapter_15-
7_%28Bible_Illustrations_by_Sweet_Media%29.jpg

There was the concept of suzerain and vassal kings in the ancient world. Vassal kings were ruled by suzerain kings from larger nations or empires. To keep the peace, they would make agreements called covenants. These covenants typically shared certain elements. Firstly, they emphasized the generosity of the suzerain king, who helped the nation of the vassal to defeat another enemy or by allowing them to live in a certain way. Next, they included curses, which were the consequences that would occur if the vassal king broke the agreement. Also included were blessings, which were the privileges the vassal king would enjoy under the suzerain rule. Lastly, there were remembrance rituals to reinforce the contract, usually done under the names or traditions of the gods of both kingdoms. This system was mirrored in the covenant system God set up with Israel after they escaped from Egypt, which is further explored in the Book of Leviticus.

Leviticus

The Levitical narrative shows the restoration of God's relationship with the people of Israel. If you trace the story back to the beginning, God dwelled among humans until the fall of Adam and Eve, caused by their disobedience. In Leviticus, God is coming full circle to dwell among the children of Israel. He commands the construction of a Tabernacle, which is like a tent temple in the middle of the desert. Once the Tabernacle was built, God dwelled within it to guide Israel.

However, Moses could not enter the Tabernacle, and the priests who went into it inappropriately died, which resulted in the institution of laws and protocols to ensure purity. Firstly, dietary laws were instituted stating what could be eaten and what could not. Secondly, states of purity were instituted according to illnesses and bodily fluids. Then, moral laws pertaining to relationships, sex, and justice were introduced. The priestly class had an even higher standard to maintain because they were the representatives of the community who stood before the Lord. These laws set a standard of what it took to remain close to God.

Most efforts are communal and focused on a relationship with the Lord, and it was noted that the concepts of clean and unclean were not necessarily the same as right and wrong. It was more about God and holding a high standard of holiness to enter His presence or to be closer to him. This thematically emphasized that a perfect God sees it fit to love people and make ways to reach out and connect with them. God began taking on a character of humility, which would later be highlighted in the narrative of Christ's sacrifice, but this was where the story began.

Numbers

The Book of Numbers focuses on the Israelite's time in the wilderness or the desert. The journey, which should have taken a couple of weeks, was extended to forty years. On the way to the Promised Land, the Israelites spent time in three main sections of the desert, namely, Mount Sinai, Paran, and Moab, on the edge of the Promised Land. Living in God's presence was started in the previous Book of Leviticus but is continued in Numbers. The Israelite camp and their traveling formation were set up with a specific emphasis on God's order and the structure of purity. When camping, the Tabernacle was in the center, surrounded by the priestly Levite tribes with the other tribes surrounding them. The Ark of the Covenant, containing God's presence, was carried in the front during travel, followed by the Levites, Judah, and the rest of the tribes. The symbolic significance of God being in the center while camping and in the front while traveling was to demonstrate that He would always be the guide.

During their travels, God always made provision for the Israelites through water, manna, and fowl so they could have meat to eat. However, despite the blessings, the Israelites always complained, stating they had enjoyed a better standard of life under the oppression of Egypt. When the cloud of God's presence moved, the Israelites were commanded to follow. Throughout their desert trek, the Israelites constantly went against their agreement with God, resulting in multiple curses, including getting attacked by snakes. How the Israelites healed from snake bites is an interesting story. A bronze snake was placed on a stake, and whenever anyone was attacked, the victim was told to look at it in order to heal. This symbolizes turning to God for your needs, and in the Christian narrative, is considered an early depiction of how Christ would be nailed to a cross for the sins of mankind.

One of the most pertinent curses was that "a generation would have to pass before they got into the Promised Land," which is why the desert journey was extended for so long. This is how the theme of balance between free will and God's will was introduced. According to the story, God wanted His people to follow Him and dwell in His presence so that He could reward them. However, God did not force this outcome. Therefore, at every step, there was a choice to reject the fellowship of God, but there would be consequences.

The theme of God transmuting evil to good was repeated in the region of Moab. As the Israelites passed through Moab to the Promised Land, the King was understandably concerned because this large nation was traveling through his territory. King Balak's concern prompted him to employ a powerful sorcerer, Balaam. Balaam recognized the unmistakable power of the God of Israel, so he prayed to Him so that he could curse the Israelites. However, Balaam found that he could only voice blessings every time he tried to curse them. The final blessing Balaam uttered was that God's promise to Abraham to bless his descendants and establish a nation would come through the leadership of a mighty Israelite king. This links the narrative back to Genesis, showing that this is one story instead of an isolated book or chapter. The transmutation of the "evil to good" theme emerged in that while the Israelites were rebelling in the valley, God was still blessing them at the top of the mountain.

Deuteronomy

The Book of Deuteronomy covers Moses's final address to the people of Israel before he died and handed over leadership to Joshua. Moses would never enter the Promised Land but brought Israel right to the edge of it. In this epic speech, Moses outlined everything Israel needed to pay attention to as they entered the Promised Land.

The Book of Deuteronomy covers Moses's final address to the people of Israel before he died and handed over leadership to Joshua.
Distant Shores Media/Sweet Publishing, CC BY-SA 3.0
<*https://creativecommons.org/licenses/by-sa/3.0*>, *via Wikimedia Commons*
https://commons.wikimedia.org/wiki/File:Book_of_Deuteronomy_Chapter_32-4_%28Bible_Illustrations_by_Sweet_Media%29.jpg

Moses opened the speech by highlighting their constant rebellion. He then transitioned into encouraging the new generation that will enter the land to not be like their ancestors but to obey God diligently. Moses reminded them about the laws of the covenant they made with God, expanding on them to make them relevant to a new generation.

One of the key revelations in Deuteronomy is the Shema, a declaration Jewish people still make today in prayer twice a day. The Shema is in Deuteronomy 6:4-5 which states, "Hear, O Israel: The Lord our God, the Lord is one. Love the Lord your God with all your heart and with all your soul and with all your strength." This is the crux of the message Moses left the Nation before his departure. Moses had to emphasize that the God of Israel is one because as they entered the Promised Land, they would dwell among a multitude of nations worshiping diverse gods. He made another statement, later echoed in the New Testament, outlining that Israel had a choice to obey and love God or rebel. Moses warned that Israel could choose death or life and continued to encourage the nation to choose life. This choice of life is a call back to the blood of the Passover lamb that freed them from Egypt.

Moses predicted that the Israelites would rebel, causing them to be exiled from the land. He concluded that this is because their hearts were hardened with selfishness and a desire to follow their own will instead of that of the Lord. To highlight that a flesh struggle is uniquely human and is deeply ingrained into the genetics of humanity, Moses linked this hardening of the heart back to the Genesis narrative when Adam and Eve fell in the Garden of Eden. However, he ended with a message of hope that the Lord would make a way to soften their hearts, which again elevated the theme of the transmutation of negative into positive. It laid the foundation for the story of Christ as a savior because, from the Christian understanding, His sacrifice opened the path for humankind to receive new hearts.

Writing Activity

Plot a visual representation of the major stories of the Torah. Explain the lessons that emerge from each story and highlight how they each link to form a grander narrative.

_____
_____
_____
_____
_____
_____
_____
_____
_____
_____
_____
_____
_____
_____
_____
_____
_____

Themes and Moral Lessons of the Torah

Thematically, the Torah reveals a few major principles. The hearts of humanity are turned to pursue wickedness. People need to work toward addressing this issue of having evil hearts by following God's commands, including rituals, laws, and festivals of remembrance. God is perfect. So, the purer you are, the closer you can get to His unfiltered presence. Although there are laws to obtain the purity that allows you to have fellowship with God, He understands that people will fall short, so he continuously shows humanity mercy throughout the narrative.

In this way, the Torah sets up the theme of humanity's constant struggle against their desires so that they can meet God's standard. Unlike teachings that promote finding yourself, the Bible is radically different. The Torah sets up the story that humanity is required to deny themselves alignment with God's desires. Suppose God is viewed as the personification of the highest good or the most righteous principles humankind can pursue. In that case, the central message of the Torah is to diminish your personal lust for a higher purpose or the spiritual mission of following God.

The communal is emphasized over the personal. Therefore, the purest people, or the priesthood, go before God to represent humanity. On the Day of Atonement, as outlined in Leviticus, a sacrifice is made where a goat is slaughtered as an offering to God, and another is set free into the wilderness carrying the sins of the community. This emphasis on forgiveness balances the justice and purity of the strict laws. Through this window of atonement, God's mercy is brought into memory to emphasize how people should engage with each other in the spirit of understanding and forgiveness. So, in addition to striving for purity in the letter of the law, love and mercy are in the heart of the Torah.

Post-Reading Activity

What lessons have you learned from each of the books of the Torah? How can some of the principles be applied in your life today?

_____
_____
_____
_____
_____
_____
_____
_____
_____
_____
_____
_____
_____
_____
_____
_____

Reflections on the Laws of the Torah and Their Modern Significance

Some laws from the Torah are known as natural laws. These emerge from cultures all over the world because they are necessary for civilization or society to sustain itself. Natural laws include principles like not lying, stealing, or murdering. In addition to these natural or moral laws, the Torah has purity laws, which are slightly different. As God descended to dwell in proximity to His people, they needed to purify themselves, which meant that some practices or conditions were considered clean or unclean.

The central message of the Torah that still rings true in the modern world is that the hearts of humanity lead them astray: Reflect on every selfish decision you or that people have made that resulted in negative outcomes. As much as people preach kindness, love, unity, forgiveness, and patience, these values seldom express themselves. A constant internal struggle aligns with these higher values against the instant gratification or easier path of selfish desires. The festivals and rituals established in the Torah bring out remembrance of God, which reminds people of the path they should walk.

Struggles and Triumphs of Biblical Characters and How They Relate to You

Throughout the Torah, you see humanity battling against their desires to follow God's ways. When the characters submit to God, they are blessed even when their backs are against the wall. When the characters rebel and turn away from God's instructions, they are cursed, bringing further hardship into their lives, but God makes a way for them to return to Him. Linked to the messages from God on curses and blessings, your obedience is always accompanied by Him, allowing you to make free choices. Still, because of His perfectly just nature, people must live with the consequences of their decisions.

When the characters submit to God, they are blessed even when their backs are against the wall.
https://pixabay.com/illustrations/grateful-thankful-appreciation-1988951/

Which of the characters in the Torah do you relate to most and why?

_____
_____
_____
_____
_____
_____
_____
_____
_____
_____
_____
_____
_____
_____
_____

How can you map their triumphs and struggles and relate them to your life? What value can you extract from your understanding?

_____
_____
_____
_____
_____
_____
_____
_____
_____
_____
_____
_____
_____
_____
_____
_____

The Shift from Scholarly to Transformative

Studying the Torah through a scholarly lens is admirable, but, in essence, these books are meant to be applied and not merely studied. Whether you are a believer or not, much wisdom can be gained from embracing the eternal truths outlined in these scriptures. Memorizing verses in the Torah and understanding the historical background can be enlightening and an excellent way to expand your knowledge. However, when the spiritual and philosophical aspects of the book are applied, only then is the scripture truly transformative. The two core messages of the Torah are that God can use your wickedness and transform it into goodness, and if you suppress your selfish desires and follow God for a higher purpose, only then will you be blessed.

How do you think you can apply some of the central themes of the Torah to transform your life?

_____
_____
_____
_____
_____
_____
_____
_____
_____
_____
_____
_____
_____
_____
_____
_____

Section 3: Books from the Old Testament

Now that you have explored the Bible's first five books, you are ready to delve into the Old Testament as a whole. This section will predominantly provide an overview of the Hebrew Bible and set the stage for more in-depth research in the subsequent sections. After studying these theoretical explanations and completing the activities, you will know how to analyze the Old Testament's literary styles and identify the major themes from the text.

The Old Testament was originally written in Hebrew.
https://www.pexels.com/photo/close-up-of-book-in-jewish-15126093/

Historical and Cultural Context of the Old Testament

The Hebrew Bible, the Tanakh, is split into three sections: the Torah, Nevi'im, and Ketuvim. The Torah or Pentateuch has been explored in the previous section. The Torah is the first five books of the Old Testament that deliver the law. The Nevi'im are the books of the prophets, and the Ketuvim can be translated as the writings. This three-part division of scripture is ancient and comes from when the texts were still recorded in scrolls. The ancient Israelites were likely to have understood the text in this way because there is a logical flow when organized like this. Furthermore, modern Jewish people who read the scriptures in the original Hebrew still use this method to divide the Old Testament.

A more contemporary division of the Old Testament groups the scriptures into categories of historical books, poetic or wisdom books, and prophetic books. The historical books encompass the Torah, Joshua, Judges, Ruth, 1 & 2 Samuel, 1 & 2 Kings, and 1 & 2 Chronicles. The poetic books are Proverbs, Psalms, Job, Song of Solomon, and Ecclesiastes. The rest of the Old Testament falls under prophetic writings, including Ezekiel, Jeremiah, Amos, and Hosea.

The Torah's themes continue throughout the rest of the Old Testament. The overarching narrative that is unveiled as the story progresses is God's relationship of love, mercy, and judgment for a people who consistently rebelled against him. The prophetic writing in the Book of Hosea encompasses this relationship well because it is compared to an adulterous marriage. Hosea was married to Gomer, a woman who continuously had extramarital affairs. According to the Torah's laws, Hosea had every right to divorce her. Instead of God telling him to abandon Gomer for her shortcomings, he tells Hosea to take her back and show her compassion, a metaphor for God's relationship with Israel. Although God is justified in abandoning his people for their worship or idols, he returns to them in His love and mercy.

It would be too extensive for scribes to write the details of every person in Israel's life, so the focus falls on three main groups – judges, kings, and prophets. When Joshua led Israel into the Promised Land, they still followed God's laws. Once Joshua died, Israel was led by a succession of judges, and the nation deteriorated once again after the Mosaic period in the wilderness. The judges of Israel were not like those you would think of in a court system. They could be more closely related to tribal chiefs. The prophets acted as the mouthpiece of God and, at different periods, revealed blessings for Israel or curses against them. However, they often concluded with a message of hope for the future as God left open a pathway for restoration and redemption.

As Israelites dwelt among the Canaanites, they worshiped the foreign gods. They tumbled down these rebellious rabbit holes so much that they became precisely like the Canaanites, so God elected to drive them out of the land. They were immoral and even practiced child sacrifice. So, God used the surrounding nations to judge Israel, eventually leading to exile from the Promised Land. Through many tumultuous occurrences, the Israelites were exiled to Babylon. The Old Testament concludes with a story of hope for the coming Messiah and the reconstruction of the temple.

Activity 1

Highlight five stories in the Old Testament where God's presence left the Israelites.

Explain why God's presence left and what had to be done to get back in alignment with God's will.

_____
_____
_____
_____
_____
_____
_____
_____
_____
_____
_____
_____
_____
_____
_____

Highlight five stories in the Old Testament where God blessed the Israelites.

_____
_____
_____
_____
_____
_____
_____
_____
_____
_____
_____
_____
_____
_____
_____

Explain how these blessings link to the theme of God's mercy and redemption and God using wickedness to transform into righteousness.

The History Books

These 17 books tell the story of humanity and Israel from creation until the fall of the Northern and Southern kingdoms. The narrative starts by showing how Israel is redeemed and saved from enslavement under the brutal rule of the pharaoh. They trace their journey through the wilderness into the Promised Land. The books detail the period of Judges, where Israel rapidly deteriorated and became like the pagan nations they replaced. Israel transitions from the period of judges into the time of kings. Internal conflicts caused the kingdom to split into northern Israel and Judah in the south. The history books of Israel conclude with the fall of both kingdoms and Israel's entry into a new captivity.

Thematic Exploration of the Old Testament through King David

The life of King David perfectly encapsulates how God blesses you when you follow his laws and how he curses you when you depart from them. It fully captures how there is always room for redemption and repentance no matter how far you have fallen and how evil can be used to ultimately facilitate righteous outcomes.

David is one of the most famous kings in the Bible, and he is rivaled only by his son, Solomon. King David's first act of heroism was defeating Goliath, a Philistine warrior everyone feared. The shepherd boy was accustomed to killing bears and wolves in the fields, so he used his skills with a slingshot to defeat the giant.

King Saul was the first ruler of Israel, but his wickedness overcame him. As David grew in popularity, King Saul became jealous and fearful, thinking David would overthrow his throne. Saul tried to kill David but failed. Through their rivalry, David's character is revealed, as he spares Saul's life continuously, even when he has easy opportunities to kill him.

David eventually ascends to the throne. He was a righteous king but also fell short. He lusted after Bathsheba, who was a married woman, entering an adulterous relationship with her. He sent Bathsheba's husband, Uriah, to the frontline of a battle to die so that he could marry her. King David succeeded in his plan, and God was disappointed in him. Nathan called out David for his wickedness, and, as judgment, the son he conceived with Bathsheba died.

A statue of King David, playing the harp.

Under David, the kingdom of Israel was strengthened and solidified. He wanted to build a temple for the Lord but did not achieve this goal. However, King Solomon, his son, built the temple David had dreamed of. Through David's line, Jesus Christ, the redeemer of Israel, was born. However, many kings who ruled after David - including Solomon - descended into wickedness and idolatry.

Activity 2

Construct a storyboard of the life of King David, noting the high and low points and the consequences. As you create this visual representation, reflect on the themes of God's justice, mercy, and duality, which exist in the heart of mankind. Include parallels to your life in your storyboard as a way to mediate deeply on the wisdom of this historical account.

_____
_____
_____
_____
_____
_____
_____
_____
_____
_____
_____
_____
_____
_____
_____
_____

The Wisdom Books

The three main wisdom books are Job, Ecclesiastes, and Proverbs. Some people include Psalms in the wisdom traditions, but the entire book does not fully match the parameters to fit into this category. The wisdom tradition opens with the Book of Proverbs. Typically, proverbs can be understood as short sayings that communicate lessons within specific cultures or groups. The Book of Proverbs contains lessons but also a narrative structure. The first part of Proverbs is presented as a father speaking to a son and guiding him. In the later part of the text, wisdom is personified as a woman and can be related to a motherly figure.

Proverbs teaches how to be wise, which in the Israelite context is not only about gaining knowledge but encompasses what you can practically apply. So, Proverbs teaches you how to live well, beginning with the fear of God so that you keep his commandments. Unlike the Mosaic law or the covenants, Proverbs makes no promises but functions with probability insofar that if you make wise decisions, positive outcomes will likely result.

Ecclesiastes throws a wrench into the mechanics of Proverbs. Although the author acknowledges it is good to live with wisdom and the fear of God, they highlight that there is no guarantee you will live well. They make this point by expressing that bad people often live great and prosperous lives, and good people often suffer. The Hebrew word encapsulating Ecclesiastes theme is "*hevel.*" Hevel is written as "meaningless" in many English translations, but a more direct translation is vapor or smoke. When you consider the qualities of smoke, you see how it maps to life.

Everything is temporary or elusive. The author of Ecclesiastes emphasizes this through the concepts of time and death. On a long enough timeline, all your achievements are meaningless. Most people have been long forgotten. On a cosmic scale, the entire existence of humanity is less than a blink. Therefore, everything you value will disappear like smoke in the wind. Death is used to illustrate the same point. Everyone meets the same end, whether wise, foolish, rich, or poor. Death is the equalizer no one can avoid. Hence, this short life on the planet is like smoke; people try to grab it, but it slips through their fingers. This seems grim, but the author concludes that the meaning of life exists in accepting this changing, paradoxical, and fleeting nature of life.

The Book of Job explores one of the most difficult questions anyone can ask. Why do bad things happen to good people? The story of Job opens with a court in heaven, where God points to Job as an example of righteousness. Satan argues that Job is only righteous because God rewards him, and if he were to remove his hedge of protection from Job, he would surely curse God. As Job falls into suffering, the theme of justice is explored through his conversations with his friends and God.

Job confesses his innocence and cries out to God to explain why all this suffering has suddenly happened to him. His friends say Job must have brought this suffering on himself because God is truly just. However, the court in heaven reveals that Job was blameless, so this cannot be the answer.

The book does not reveal why bad things happen to good people but puts humanity's place in the cosmos into perspective. God reveals to Job that complicated structures hold the universe together, and his finite mind could not possibly understand it. Therefore, Job is not able to question God's justice. The answer God provides about why good things happen to bad people is that it is far too complicated for a human to comprehend. Job humbles himself and repents in this realization, and God gifts him back everything he lost. This ties into Ecclesiastes insofar as people must accept what they cannot control or explain. When the wisdom books are viewed through the lens of the extended Old Testament theme of the cycle of justice, curses, and redemption, they reveal that it is not as simple as mere surface-level analysis, so trusting in God is vital.

Activity 3

Consider the Proverb's central message to live well according to scriptural principles. Consider Job's message to humble yourself before God. Now, reflect on the wisdom of Ecclesiastes to let go of control and accept what God gives you.

How can you apply these themes to your life as it currently stands?

Prophetic Writings

One central message is delivered to Israel by every prophet, even though the specifics of their lives teach unique lessons. Every prophet delivered the message that God should be worshipped – *and God alone* – in order to be blessed.

Or you can rebel and face God's judgment.

Israel's history reflects this message as they prospered and fell. The prophets always followed the same structure in their writings. First, they called out the sins of the people. Then, they asked the people to return to God's laws. Lastly, they warned the people of the judgment they would suffer in the event of their rebellion.

One of the more unique prophets was Jonah because he was controversial. The Book of Jonah ends on a cliffhanger with God asking a question that Jonah does not answer. Jonah's character is already in question because he prophesied that a wicked king, Jeroboam II, would succeed and gain territory. At the same time, Amos, another prophet of God, gave the opposite message, saying the king would lose it all due to his wickedness.

The Book of Jonah sets up the extension of salvation to the gentile nations and encapsulates the Old Testament theme of the transformation of evil into good. Jonah was an Israelite and of God's people. However, he disobeyed God, and the pagans he met obeyed God. God sent Jonah to the Ninevites to tell them their city would be overturned. However, Jonah fled in the opposite direction, ending up on a pagan boat. When a storm approached, Jonah was thrown overboard, and the pagans repented and worshiped God, highlighting the transformation of Jonah's wickedness into the positive outcome of winning souls to worship the true God. Jonah was swallowed by a whale, and God allowed him to follow through with his mission. Jonah reluctantly delivered the prophecy to the Ninevites. Jonah fled not out of fear but because he hated the Ninevites and wanted them destroyed.

Jonah was swallowed by a whale, and God allowed him to follow through with the mission.

After the Ninevites repented and God spared them, Jonah was miserable. God sent Jonah a vine for shade, which cheered him up. God reversed the blessing by sending a worm to kill the vine, causing Jonah to wish for death. God brought to Jonah's attention how he is mourning the vine that gave him shade. God asked Jonah if he was willing to mourn a vine – *and how much more were the Ninevites worth?* Then, God asked Jonah if it was not worth it for God to give them a chance. Jonah did not answer, causing the reader to reflect on what it means for God to forgive their enemies. The forgiveness of enemies and using Jonah, who hated the Ninevites, again expresses the theme of God transforming wickedness into righteousness.

Activity 4

1. Choose one Old Testament prophet.
2. Summarize their story.
3. List the prophecies, warnings, and judgments they delivered.
4. Write about the lessons that can be learned from this account.
5. How does the prophet you chose link to the Old Testament themes of judgment, redemption, obedience to God, and using evil to bring about good?

_____
_____
_____
_____

The Covenantal System

A covenant is widely understood as a promise, but a more accurate way of looking at it is as a contract. God creates agreements with His people to bless them if they align to a certain standard and warns of the consequences of departing from those standards. In the Old Testament, there are four covenants before the fifth and final covenant of the New Testament under the sacrifice of Christ. The covenantal system includes the Noahic, Abrahamic, Mosaic, and Davidic covenants.

The Noahic covenant is the first in line. After flooding the world and ridding the planet of a wicked generation, God promised Noah that humanity would continue and that He would never destroy the Earth by water again. At the end of God's wrath and justice, mercy emerged in this Genesis account.

The next covenant comes through Abraham and is probably one of the most significant because it results in the birth of three major world religions: Judaism, Christianity, and Islam. God institutes the practice of circumcision, and for his faithfulness, God promises Abraham a nation and that the world would be blessed through his seed. God also promised that his people would receive land in which their nation could thrive.

The Mosaic covenant is the institution of the Law of Moses. As God delivered the Israelites out of Egyptian captivity, he gave them a law to govern their lives morally and ceremonially. The agreement was that if they were obedient, they would be blessed, and if they disobeyed, they would be cursed. The history of the Israelite people is framed through this lens of blessings and curses and a central theme of the Old Testament.

The last covenant before the coming of the Messiah, who saved humanity through grace and faith, is the Davidic promise, which is a continuation of the Mosaic Law. God promised to maintain the Israelites in the land if they obeyed Him but warned that they would go into exile if they departed from His ways and worshiped foreign gods. God also promised that a Messiah would come through the line of David, which would be the redemption of a fallen Israel.

Activity 5

Write down the details of each covenant and outline how it ties into the eventual coming of the Messiah in the New Testament.

_____
_____
_____
_____
_____
_____
_____
_____
_____
_____
_____
_____
_____
_____
_____

Section 4: Wisdom Literature: Proverbs, Psalms, and Parables

The Bible is a multifaceted collection of books containing prophecies, law, history, mysteries, and practical wisdom. The wisdom literature deals less with grand revelations and more with the everyday lives of humans. As much as the details of the law can be understood, and the miracles of the text can be marveled at, they are sometimes not practically grounded. Therefore, the wisdom traditions of the scriptures provide a human perspective of work, family, and relationships as a way to navigate the complexities of the trials and triumphs resulting from life.

The books of Psalms, Proverbs, and Ecclesiastes, the parables of the Bible, give unique teachings in the wisdom tradition. These texts have common threads but differing perspectives, enabling the books to appeal to people in different stages of their lives with varying mindsets. These teachings are easy to understand because they are written to make them relatable to people. Although the texts were composed within a historical and cultural context, the messages they teach are relevant because some aspects of the human condition do not change.

Exploring the wisdom texts will give you an in-depth understanding of each book and how they emerged. You will learn how they applied to the people at the time, but, more importantly, you will reflectively engage with them so that they can be brought alive and grasped more deeply by interpreting them as practical and applicable guides. In this way, you can establish a link to the past by introspectively analyzing the text through the lens of your experience in the present. By relating the scriptures to your life, the wisdom books unfold into their fullness, allowing you to better embody the mentality of the authors and the audience they were speaking to.

Psalms

The Book of Psalms is a compilation of prayers, poems, and songs. Some works are anonymous, but different parts of the texts are attributed to various authors. Seventy-three Psalms are attributed to King David, a skilled poet and musician. One reason King David grew so close to Saul was his ability to soothingly play the harp. Other Psalms are attributed to Asaph, the sons of Korah, and the worship leaders of the temple, Heman and Ethan. Many texts in Psalms were sung as worship songs but not exclusively as hymns. The primary motivation for compiling the Psalms was to hold onto the spiritual traditions of Israel during the Babylonian exile. Therefore, the Book of Psalms emphasizes how Israelites should live in faith so that they can return to the Promised Land.

The Book of Psalms is a compilation of prayers, poems, and songs.

Psalms can be logically divided into six sections, the first two Psalms being an introduction, encouraging meditation on the Torah's teachings, and reiterating the Messianic covenant established with King David.

Psalms 3 to 41 deal with covenantal faithfulness. Themes of blessings, curses, and mercy emerge as a constant thread in the Old Testament. In this section, you find one of the most popular texts in the Bible, Psalm 23:1, "The Lord is my shepherd, I shall not be in want." This Psalm emphasizes the reliance on God and total commitment to Him that Moses expressed in Deuteronomy 6:4-5 "Hear, O Israel: The Lord our God, the Lord is one. Love the Lord your God with all your heart and with all your soul and with all your strength."

The next grouping is Psalms 42-72, which expresses the hope for a coming Messiah after the exile the Israelites were experiencing. They depict how the Psalms' authors and compilers recognized that their captivity resulted from the wickedness that they embraced in the Promised Land – but that they held onto a brighter future in the new Messianic kingdom. This section concludes with Psalms 72: 1-2, "Endow the king with your justice, O God, the royal son with your righteousness. May he judge your people in righteousness, your afflicted ones with justice." This verse describes the institution of a Messianic kingdom. Notice the repetition of the word "*justice*," a literary device used by the poetry of Psalms. When Psalms' authors wanted to emphasize an idea, they often used repeating words.

The next section of Psalms spans from chapters 73 to 89, which outlines a hope for the coming of the Messiah amid the exile of the Israelites. Psalm 73:1 says, "Surely God is good to Israel, to those who are pure in heart." This may seem strange considering that Israel was under brutal Babylon rule, but it was a cry of hope that their liberation was near following the coming of a Messiah. Many of the Psalms compiled were written by David as a reminder of the promise God made to him to deliver a righteous king from his bloodline. The Israelites, under their oppression, needed to keep this hope of salvation coming through the bloodline of David alive. The Psalms compilation was created to allow the promises to resonate in the Israelites' collective memory. Psalms 90 to 106 emphasize God as the King of creation, instilling hope that the Israelites were in His hands and that He had the power to take them out of their oppression. Psalms 107-150 conclude the book with songs of praise.

The poetry of Psalms has a unique reflection style. Firstly, it draws back to some themes used in the earlier books, but it also interestingly mirrors itself. This mirroring is done by repeating words, like in Psalm 29:5, "The voice of the Lord breaks the cedars; the Lord breaks in pieces the cedars of Lebanon." The breaking of cedars is repeated for emphasis. A similar technique is employed to repeat ideas instead of words, like in Psalm 40:8, "I desire to do your will, my God; your law is within my heart." The idea of following God's will is repeated by highlighting the desire to do what the Lord wants. This is done by the author saying the law is in their heart and they want to do God's will, which is the same idea expressed in different words. This mirroring or repetition creates a unique poetic flow, allowing essential ideas to jump out at the reader using parallel pairings.

The ideas of redemption, hope, faith, the destruction of enemies, and the renewal of the glory of Israel through submitting to God are the key ideas of Psalms, expressed through beautiful poetic writing. Considering the historical context of this book's compilation of the Israelites in Babylonian exile, it makes sense that they would choose songs and poetry to communicate these ideas. The authors wanted the readers to memorize the texts to embody these principles. Hence, poetry was a better avenue than intense historical or narrative writing.

By poetically engaging with these ideas, the author gives the reader an entertaining and engaging way to grasp more profound teachings. Psalms is a brilliant book for a beginner to engage with scripture. Its practical nature and poetic language to emphasize key ideas make understanding easier than more complex prophetic doctrines requiring a baseline understanding of the law and the covenantal system. As part of the wisdom tradition, the Psalms dive more into everyday occurrences and classic wisdom that can be understood by people outside the culture, including believers and non-believers.

Activity 1

Write a poem exploring some ideas of Psalms relevant to your life. Draw on other writings of the Old Testament and use the poetic techniques employed in the book to emphasize your main message.

Proverbs

This intriguing book is one of the most defining scriptures for understanding Biblical wisdom. Most of the writings in Proverbs are attributed to Solomon. However, some are considered a collection of cultural knowledge predating the king. In addition to King Solomon, writings in Proverbs are attributed to Agur, son of Jakeh, and King Lemuel. The book is intertwined with the concept of wisdom, and Solomon's character is significant because, in 2 Chronicles 1:10, Solomon asks the Lord for wisdom so that he can lead his people well. Therefore, the king was intrinsically linked with this theme.

The Book of Proverbs was likely completed under the United Kingdoms of Israel during the 10th century BC. However, the compilation may have occurred later after the split, with the book being completed in the Southern Kingdom of Judah. Considering the cultural wisdom chain related to Solomon, some aspects of ancient Mesopotamia and Egypt also come out in the text. The personification of abstract ideas, like wisdom and folly indicative of the Proverbs writing, is a motif embedded in these ancient regions that may have influenced the writing style. If you consider the historical development of the religious idea of the Near East, then this amalgamation and cross-contamination is not surprising. The spiritual traditions of Israel were not birthed in a vacuum but came from common understandings and interwoven regional influences.

The Book of Proverbs specifically addresses young men, but timeless wisdom can be applied to people across time and cultural spectrums. Proverbs urges young men to decide wisely by basing their lives on submission to the will of God. Young men face two major temptations of folly according to Proverbs: the enticement to exploit people for wealth and falling into sexual immorality with women outside of wedlock.

Since ancient Israel practiced a collectivist culture, many of the wisdom teachings of Proverbs are framed through this communal understanding. The text teaches about having love for friends and the community and avoiding the exploitation of the most vulnerable in society, like widows, orphans, and the poor. There is a governmental element to the wisdom because Proverbs speaks about not using the courts or official structures to oppress people.

Proverbs is practical in its advice, outlining the perspective a young man should have if he wants to live a happy and fulfilling life. Proverbs highlights that a happy life is only found in the service of God. In addition to being happy, Proverbs emphasizes that living in submission to God is the only way to be useful. This extends through the Israelite understanding that conforming to the ways of God brings blessings, and departing from them brings curses.

Proverbs continues to clarify that God is not exclusively for Israel, but His wisdom extends throughout the world. This is why many of the teachings in Proverbs are also found in Mesopotamian and Egyptian schools of thought. The author purposely does this to emphasize that wise teachings are not merely confined to temples but should permeate every aspect of life. Proverbs is an early example of removing religious traditions from ceremonial practice, emphasizing that it is a way of life.

The community aspect of Proverbs is not limited to helping the vulnerable but comes forth in how it encourages young men to work hard and be humble. The wisdom tradition of Proverbs teaches that praise for your character and work should not come from yourself but should be invoked by those around you. It discourages laziness so that you can be a functional member of your community and contribute diligently.

Activity 2

Read the Book of Proverbs. Write a poem or short story that personifies wisdom and folly in your life as you reflect on the scripture's guidance.

_____

_____

_____

_____

_____

_____

The communal aspect of the wisdom of Proverbs is clear. How do you think official structures and social contracts exploit the most vulnerable in society today? How can it be avoided or remedied?

Ecclesiastes

Of all the wisdom writings, the Book of Ecclesiastes is uniquely naturalistic.

Of all the wisdom writings, the Book of Ecclesiastes is uniquely naturalistic. The text is written in a way that acknowledges the complexities of the human condition and reveals profound truths about reality through this exploration. From the viewpoint of God, or human idealism, the world seems solid and should be fair. The wisdom books of Proverbs and Psalms emphasize the importance of making wise decisions for favorable outcomes. Ecclesiastes shatters that idealism with a dose of dark reality. No matter what you do, nothing is certain.

Regardless of what you seek in this earthly realm, it is all obsolete. Ecclesiastes explains that for the pleasure seekers, their moments of ecstasy pass, and misery will return at some point. Those who pursue wealth will exchange all their time for riches and may never get to spend it until they are too old to enjoy it. Then, they leave their inheritance to those who may have no interest in it. The Ecclesiastes author emphasizes that even the pursuit of knowledge is vain because the more you know, the more your sorrow increases since you now see the intricacies of the wickedness in the world.

This seems like a gloomy, nihilistic setup, but it is only to prepare the stage for the message of the entire Bible captured within this short book:

God is sovereign over all. Attempting to control the world and manipulate the outcomes of life is a fool's errand. The author acknowledges that it is preferred to follow the practical wisdom of Psalms and Proverbs but acknowledges that this does not guarantee anything. Like Job, who experienced difficulties despite being blameless, you must recognize that the Creator is sovereign.

Through all the highs and lows of being human, death knocks on everyone's door. The simple message to overcome the meaninglessness and unfairness of life is to keep God's commandments and fear Him. In this way, you take the burden of working out the complexities and paradoxes of life out of your hands and place that burden at the feet of the only one who could possibly understand, the Most High.

An artistic depiction of Death.

Ecclesiastes is about understanding human limitations in a vast and confusing world. As much as people try to maintain the illusion of control, only God's grace brings them blessings, His mercy sustains them, and His judgment tears them down from high places. Centering a life on acknowledging that only God is in control is the Biblical concept of fearing God, repeated throughout the Old and New Testaments.

Often, people feel that their efforts get them to their position in life, but they forget that God's mercy is above the works of their own hands. Imagine a man who gets rich by carving intricate designs into furniture. He is highly respected, and his artwork is sought after by celebrities and politicians all over the world. He put in endless hours of practice and marketing to reach his current level. On the way home from a networking meeting, he gets into a tragic car accident and loses both his hands. All the hours spent perfecting his craft are now meaningless, and he must find a new way to earn an income. Regardless of his efforts, it is only God who gifted him the ability to prosper. As all his blessings came, God can take them away in an instant for reasons beyond human comprehension. The only constant that would make sense during and after the success is to honor God because He is in control. This is the core of Ecclesiastes' message.

Activity 3

List as many of your achievements in life as you can remember.

List as many of your failures as you can remember.

_____
_____
_____
_____
_____
_____
_____
_____
_____
_____
_____
_____
_____
_____
_____

Reflect on how temporary these experiences are.

_____
_____
_____
_____
_____
_____
_____
_____
_____
_____
_____
_____
_____
_____

Think about how much of what occurs in your life you can control and how much is beyond your control.

_____
_____
_____
_____
_____
_____
_____
_____
_____
_____
_____
_____
_____
_____
_____
_____

Through the lens of God's sovereignty, write about aspects of your life you should let go so that you can be guided by trust in a higher power.

_____
_____
_____
_____
_____
_____
_____
_____
_____
_____
_____
_____
_____
_____
_____
_____
_____

Parables

Teaching using parables is an ancient technique spanning cultures and times. Jesus is most well-known in the Bible for using parables to convey his message, allowing it to contextually resonate with His audience. However, the Messiah was drawing a long Israelite tradition of using metaphor to communicate powerful lessons.

The Biblical parable is structured in two parts. The first is the "*mashal*," when a short and engaging story is told. The second is the reveal, the "*nimshal*," the explanation allowing the audience to understand the parable. An example of this parable structure is when Jotham addressed the people of Shechem in Judges 9:7-15, referring to trees choosing a king among them. Jotham completes the parable in Judges 9:16-20 by comparing the imagery to the current political situation of the Shechem people.

Nathan uses this same parable structure when he rebukes King David for the wickedness he committed against Uriah by having an adulterous relationship with Bathsheba. Nathan started by telling the story of a rich man who stole the only lamb his neighbor had. David confidently stated how he believed that this terrible person deserved to be put to death. Nathan then revealed the nimshal by remarking that David was this wicked man, causing the king to repent.

Activity 4

Choose one of the consistent themes of the Old Testament. Use the structure of the mashal, followed by the nimshal, to construct a parable to communicate this scriptural theme. Use symbols and tropes in the parable that will make it relevant to a modern audience in contemporary times.

Section 5: The Prophetic Voices: Isaiah to Malachi

When people think of scripture, prophecy is probably the first thing that comes to mind. The Abrahamic traditions revere messages from prophets who act as God's mouthpiece on Earth. During the history of Israel, they went through specific social or political events. God communicated through prophets to address the people according to what occurred in the land. Prophets often referenced a future period where redemption or judgment would happen.

What Is Prophecy?

An accurate description of prophecy would be the message that God delivers to his people.
https://pixabay.com/illustrations/bible-prophecy-cross-christianity-2062081/

People mistake prophecy for fortune-telling. Prophets tell of events that will occur in the future in the Bible, but this does not align with the scriptural understanding of prophecy. A prophet is like an ambassador for God, so a more accurate description of prophecy would be the message God delivers to his people. God works through a set order. What he communicates must flow through a hierarchy. Typically, God delivers a message to a prophet, which they will convey to the leadership or the masses, depending on the desires of the Most High.

Common Themes of Prophetic Messages

The minor and major prophets emphasize that God is sovereign over all. They come to warn people of a coming judgment due to their disobedience, injustice, and idol worship. Although many prophecies of the Old Testament contain terrifying warnings and descriptions of the wrath of God that could cause a person's heart to stop, they also come with possible redemption. God does not punish His people in vain. Every time Israel or other nations were judged, it was for them to repent of their wicked ways and return to righteousness. The narrative continued throughout the Bible, which is that God is making a way for His people to be redeemed, but it is balanced with justice because God's perfect mercy and fairness must be expressed.

Symbology of Prophecy

Common symbolic images emerge when Biblical prophecy is studied. Prophets often compare governments, nations, or key figures to beasts, emphasizing the carnal and destructive nature that the unjust take. Another repeated symbol that emerges is adultery or prostitution because grasping the covenantal system is easier than a marriage contract. A husband and wife commit to each other and make certain vows, and the rejection of extramarital affairs is one of the central tenets. Similarly, God commits to his people that He will bless and care for them, but they must follow his commandments and not worship idols or foreign gods.

Like a marriage destroyed by infidelity, God's relationship with His people is broken when they sway from their promises. However, God is like a forgiving husband who is merciful and always presents the opportunity for repentance so that His people can be redeemed. In apocalyptic writing, profound, esoteric symbolism is often used because prophets could not be found speaking out against empires and risking death. So, they had to keep their writings' meanings under wraps to allow only a select group to understand the text.

Major Prophets

The difference between major and minor prophets is not their importance but the length of the scrolls that refer to the details of their lives and prophecies. There are four major prophets and twelve minor prophets. The scriptures mention the existence of other prophets who spoke for the God of Israel and the gods of other nations, but they are not referred to by name. A prophet's position was taken on by many in the ancient world and was an important seat to fill. Since prophets were the mouthpieces of God, it is understandable why the Biblical text was concerned with separating false prophets from authentic ones.

Isaiah

Isaiah.

Missional Volunteer, CC BY-SA 2.0 <https://creativecommons.org/licenses/by-sa/2.0>, via Wikimedia Commons https://commons.wikimedia.org/wiki/File:Isaiah_%281%29.jpg

Isaiah is one of the most significant prophets because of the messages he delivered about the coming Messiah. The nation of Judah had turned away from God when Isaiah was most active between 739 BC and 681 BC. They focused on ceremonial symbols and sacrifices but had completely abandoned the heart of the law. The people in Judah had become harsh and treated the kingdom's vulnerable with contempt. They had no love or kindness in their hearts, so their sacrifices were meaningless. Isaiah offered the most complete prophecies of a coming Messiah, who Christians believe was fulfilled by Jesus. His prophecies mentioned a virgin birth, and the child would be called Immanuel, which translates to "God with us." Isaiah highlighted Judah's lack of love, which was restored and fulfilled by the arrival of Christ.

Jeremiah

Jeremiah.
Giorgio Ghisi, CC0, via Wikimedia Commons
https://commons.wikimedia.org/wiki/File:The_Prophet_Jeremiah,_from_the_series_of_Prophets_and_Sibyls_in_the_Sistine_Chapel_MET_DP821566.jpg

The books of Jeremiah and Lamentations are linked to this powerful prophet. Jeremiah functioned in the decades leading to the fall of Judah and their 70-year captivity in Babylon. By using the metaphor of adultery and prostitution, Jeremiah explained how Judah abandoned God by worshipping idols. Furthermore, Jeremiah prophesied that Judah's leaders were corrupt and oppressed the poor, widows, orphans, and immigrants. Therefore, God used Babylon to judge the Israelites. Although Babylon was an evil empire, God used them to judge Israel, revealing the recurring Biblical theme of God transforming wickedness into righteousness. Jeremiah's warnings of judgment came to pass, which facilitated the Book of Lamentations, which recorded the events of the Babylonian exile and attributed the exile to their sin. Lamentations expressed Judah's grief and concluded with their repentance and hope for the future.

Ezekiel

Ezekiel.
Giorgio Ghisi, CC0, via Wikimedia Commons

Under Nebuchadnezzar II's leadership, Babylon had begun taking over Judah during Ezekiel's prophecies. As a priest, Ezekiel was captured because of his high rank and kept as a servant in the city of Tel-Abib. As a vassal to the Empire of Babylon, Judah yearned for freedom, hoping to emerge victorious by collaborating with their Egyptian neighbors. On the Chebar riverbanks, Ezekiel received a vision of Israel's judgment and its neighbors, with Babylon as the tool God used. Ezekiel saw the presence of God leaving the temple in Jerusalem because of idolatry and corruption. However, he prophesied hope that God would redeem his people and restore the temple. The powerful imagery of dry bones lying in the desert depicts the current spiritual condition of God's people, and then the bones being restored with flesh depicts rebirth and restoration through God's redemption of His people. Ezekiel was a forerunner of apocalyptic traditions, making prophecies about the end times that were later repeated in the book of Revelations.

Daniel

Daniel.
Ted, Attribution-ShareAlike 2.0 Generic, CC BY-SA 2.0 DEED

Daniel, alongside other young men, was a captive of King Nebuchadnezzar. He prophesied when Judah was oppressed in Babylon for 70 years, as Jeremiah foretold. Daniel's faith remained strong throughout his life. As a teenager, Daniel was trained among the aristocracy of Babylon. His ability to interpret dreams won him favor from King Nebuchadnezzar and the rulers that followed. Jealousy among the elites got him thrown into a lion's den, but he emerged unscathed as a sign he was anointed. Daniel's prophecies used terrifying imagery of beasts to foretell about the kingdoms that would dominate the world and the events of the end times. Daniel's end-time prophecies relate to imageries in Revelations with the coming of the antichrist and the establishment of God's eternal kingdom that will rule over all other kingdoms.

Minor Prophets

The texts of the Minor Prophets are shorter than the Major Prophets but are not less important. The central message of prophecy is reinforced in these books. The theme of God blessing Israel when they keep His commandments and punishing them when they become unjust, unloving, and idolatrous is repeated in these short texts. It is unclear why more was revealed to some prophets and less to others, but the messages they delivered hold equal importance because they still come from God in the Biblical narrative. The symbolism used in the lives of the Minor Prophets communicates powerful messages. It clarifies the themes extended throughout the pages of the Old Testament, starting with the initial foundation of the Torah.

Hosea

Hosea.

This prophet began his work when Israel had already split into two kingdoms. Hosea operated in the Northern Kingdom. Hosea delivered prophecies of harsh condemnation by rebuking the elites who oppressed the poor and vulnerable and called out the idol worship of Israel. The Lord used Hosea's life as a symbol of how He interacted with Israel. Hosea's wife, Gomer, was a promiscuous woman. However, God did not call the prophet to rebuke her. God does the opposite, instructing Hosea to reconcile and have children expressing symbolic representation of God's relationship with His people. Even though they broke the covenant and metaphorically had adulterous relationships with other gods, the Lord still held faithful to his side of the covenant, ensuring that after judgment and turmoil, Israel would be redeemed.

Joel

Joel.
Giorgio Ghisi, CC0, via Wikimedia Commons
https://commons.wikimedia.org/wiki/File:The_Prophet_Joel,_from_the_series_of_Prophets_and_Sibyls_in_the_Sistine_Chapel_MET_DP821553.jpg

Joel was a prophet whose name meant "Yahweh is God." The prophet was active around 835 BC. When Joel came into the picture, the southern kingdom of Judah was in free fall economically, socially, and spiritually. When Joel was ministering, Judah experienced a devastating plague of locusts that ravaged the already struggling kingdom. Joel used this plague to highlight that worse was yet to come if Judah did not change its ways. He reinforced the idea that previous prophets mentioned how the Lord uses natural disasters and invading armies to judge nations that practice wickedness. Like many other prophets, Joel ended with a message of hope that all is not lost – *and calamity can be avoided.* He emphasized that if the people repent and return to the ways of the Lord, He will bless them, and they will not meet the tragic end that many other nations had decades prior.

Amos

Amos.
Ted, Attribution-ShareAlike 2.0 Generic CC BY-SA 2.0 DEED

The prophet Amos's ministry was short-lived, lasting less than a year in 760 BC. Israel had already been divided into two kingdoms, and

Amos was from Judah. Amos was not recognized as a professional prophet in the religious structures but worked as a farmer. Since Amos did not belong to the religious structures, it allowed him to openly prophesize against them. He pointed out their hypocrisy because they observed rituals and ceremonies but exploited the poor to build their wealth. Judah was still small and was not yet threatened by bigger nations. Amos condemned Israel and their neighbors for their treatment of the poor, saying their injustice was a sign that they rejected God despite how they appeared outwardly holy.

Obadiah

Obadiah.

There is not much known about Obadiah's life. Due to the name being quite common, other mentions of the name Obadiah cannot accurately be linked to this prophet. Obadiah delivered his prophecy when both kingdoms had fallen, and Israel was in Babylonian exile. The Lord's judgment of Israel was clear, and the people mourned and repented. However, Obadiah preached hope by letting the people know their captivity was not the end. He prophesied that the day of the Lord was still to come, and the nations would be judged. He continued proclaiming that Israel would be restored, giving the broken people something to look forward to. Obadiah's prophecies highlighted that a merciful God would give his people another chance and open a pathway for redemption after judgment.

Jonah

Jonah was a rebellious prophet. The Book of Jonah is short, but it is one of the most popular stories in the Bible. Jonah tries to run from the prophecy he is meant to deliver to the Ninevites. However, his fleeing is futile because the Lord is in charge of the Earth. As he tried to escape, a storm ravaged the ship he was on. The pagans prayed to the God of Israel, and He revealed that Jonah was the reason for the turmoil. They threw Jonah overboard upon the prophet's request, and they repented. A big fish swallowed Jonah, and in its stomach, Jonah prayed for salvation and promised to complete the mission. Through the story of Jonah's rebellion, God teaches that even pagan nations can be redeemed, and this lays the foundation for the message of loving your enemies, which was later preached by Christ.

Micah

Micah began his ministry in 721 BC. Israel had already split into the northern kingdom of Israel and Judah in the south. Micah predicted the fall of the northern kingdom. This prophet was a mysterious figure because not much is known about his life, and the Book of Micah does not present a narrative about his personal experiences. The prophet predicted the eventual fall of Judah, but he assumed it would be a lot earlier. Some central themes of Micah are the condemnation of false prophets and the rebuke of wayward leadership. Micah emphasizes that because Israel represents God's chosen people, it does not mean they are free from the consequences of their actions. Micah stated it is misleading to preach hope to the people when they are storing up God's wrath. Prophesying should be with God's timing, reaffirming the theme of the Lord's sovereignty.

Nahum

Nahum.
PravoslavnyChristianin, CC0, через Викисклад
https://commons.wikimedia.org/wiki/File:Prophet_Nahum.webp?uselang=ru

The Book of Jonah and the Book of Nahum work hand in hand. When Jonah warns the Ninevites that their city may be overturned, causing them to repent and be redeemed by God, Nahum prophesies their destruction. Nahum preached that the Lord is slow to anger, but like Judah and Israel were judged by the Lord, the Assyrians would face the same treatment. Ninevah's witchcraft and harlotry brought down God's wrath upon them. Nahum described in detail how the city would fall, and within 20 years of his prophecies, the events came to pass when the Babylonians destroyed the once mighty region. Nahum showed that God does not rule over Israel exclusively. He is the God of *the world,* reestablishing the Biblical theme of the Lord's sovereignty.

Habakkuk

Habakkuk.

The height of Habakkuk's ministry was near the tail end of Judah before the kingdom fell. At this point, the Israelites in Judah became like the surrounding nations, partaking in idolatry and oppressing its most vulnerable citizens. Habakkuk was unique because he did not address Israel or its leadership. Instead, he conversed directly with God. Habakkuk struggled to understand whether God was truly good because of the injustice He allowed in Judah. God responded to Habakkuk, telling him that he would use Babylon to judge Israel, to which the prophet was appalled because the Babylonians were even worse. However, God reassured Habakkuk of His just nature by revealing that Babylon would also get judged for its actions. The main message that God gets through to Habakkuk is that he should trust the Lord entirely because He is just and sovereign.

Zephaniah

Zephaniah.

Zephaniah traces his lineage back to Hezekiah, but other than this detail, little is known about this prophet. Zephaniah prophesied during the Josiah reign, who would be the 16th king of Judah around 640 BC to 609 BC. The prophet was probably active during the early part of King Josiah's reign because Assyria and Nineveh are mentioned in the book, but Babylon is omitted, so they may not yet have been a major threat to the southern kingdom. In the tradition of the prophets before him, Zephaniah noticed Judah straying from the ways of the Lord and warned of a coming judgment if they did not repent. Zephaniah also spoke of the day of the Lord, where there would be mass destruction, considered an end-times prophecy.

Haggai

Haggai's ministry began when a group of Israelites returned to Judah after the 70-year exile in Babylon. Cyrus of Persia defeated the Babylonians and allowed some Judaens to return home under the Persian-appointed governor's leadership of Zerubbabel. Haggai had a vision of the restoration of the temple that was destroyed during the Babylonian conquest. Within five years, the temple was rebuilt and dedicated to the Most High. The reconstruction of the temple under the prophecies of Haggai demonstrates that after judgment comes redemption.

Zechariah

Zechariah.

A central point of Zechariah's prophecies is the sovereignty of the Lord, a common thread throughout the Bible and foundational to an Israelite worldview. Zechariah opened the view of the Israelite God as sovereign over all nations and called everyone to submit to Him. This was revolutionary in the ancient world, where gods were viewed as being dedicated to specific geographical regions, and at some point, the Israelite God was understood in the same way. Many consider Zechariah's work as a foreshadowing of the coming Messiah that would open the final covenant beyond the Israelites and to the Gentiles.

Malachi

Malachi, like Haggai, functioned during the Israelite's return from Babylonian exile. This prophet spoke out against the behavior of the Israelite leadership, more specifically, the Levitical priesthood. Many priests became decadent and indulgent, offering inferior sacrifices to the Lord, which could be traced back to Cain in Genesis, whom the Lord rebuked for not offering the first of his harvest. Furthermore, Malachi spoke against intermarrying with women from other nations who worshiped foreign gods, resulting in divorces being common. Malachi also called for the people to tithe more effectively because it was considered a doorway to blessings. Malachi highlighted Elijah as a forerunner for the Messiah and preached about the end times or the day of the Lord.

Relevance of Prophecy in the Modern World

When you study the prophecies delivered to Israel, its leaders, and those given to other nations, certain messages are repeated. According to scripture, due to the fall of humanity, it is likely that people will stray from the path God has set out for them. So, the same sins the Israelites embraced in the past – injustice and idol worship – will reemerge in contemporary times. Today, the world is becoming less religious, so it may not be clear what idols are in the contemporary age. However, the worship of material goods and the reverence of celebrities have replaced the Babylonian gods with whom the Israelites were enticed. Furthermore, there is mass injustice on Earth, with many of the rich exploiting the poor, keeping them in an oppressive cycle of poverty. Therefore, the prophetic message of the men of God is as relevant today as it was centuries ago.

Group Activity

Discuss in a group of four or five how the prophecies warning against idolatry and injustice and calling for repentance are relevant in the world today.

Journal Activity

Write down how the call for repentance, the warnings of the consequences of idol worship, and straying from the commandments of God are relevant in your life. Lamentations is a book of mourning and repentance. Include in your journal what you think you should turn away from and repent for.

_____
_____
_____
_____
_____
_____
_____
_____
_____
_____
_____
_____
_____
_____
_____
_____

Section 6: Dissecting the Gospels

The Gospels culminate the narratives established in the Torah, which continued in the historic, wisdom, and prophetic writings. God set up a covenantal system of laws, ceremonies, and celebrations. Central to this system was the practice of sacrifice. Many sacrifices exist in the Israelite tradition, but one of the most important was the Day of Atonement. This prestigious religious day has a whole chapter dedicated to it in the book of Leviticus. The Israelites became defiled throughout the year through their sins. So, on the Day of Atonement, a sacrifice was offered with the blood of an animal to cleanse the community.

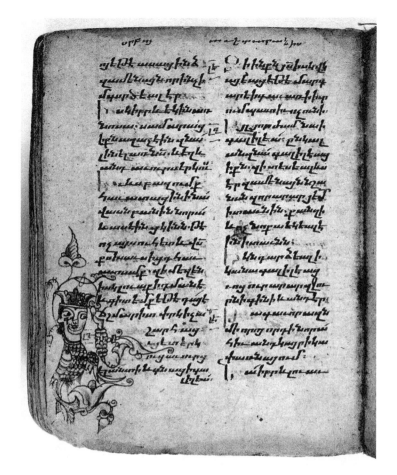

The Gospels culminate the narratives established in the Torah, which continued in the historic, wisdom, and prophetic writings.

Two goats were used in the ritual. The first goat was slaughtered and offered to God as a payment for the debt of the Israelite sin. A second goat that took on the sins of the community was released into the wilderness as a symbol of the transgressions of the year being carried away. The second animal, known as a scapegoat, is where the popular English literary phrase originates. For the Israelites to be forgiven, an eternal sacrifice was needed. Therefore, Christ came to fulfill that blueprint so that all people, at all times, could be washed clean of their sins.

Gospel is translated as good news or a good story. In Christian understanding, the crux of the good news is that Christ sacrificed Himself so that whoever believes in Him their sins could be redeemed. Most Christians believe that Christ is the Son of God and God in the flesh. To justify this position, they point to various New Testament references from Jesus's words and the apostles' teachings. They also point to Old Testament prophecies. Therefore, for believers, God establishes a new covenant, allowing all the nations to dwell in His presence through the sacrifice of His Son.

Historical Contexts of the Gospels

The church came before the written Gospel. Before the text was scribed, it was preached through oral traditions. These teachings were circulated among the early underground church, which was persecuted by the Roman authorities and some Israelite religious leaders. The Levitical priesthood once acted as a bridge connecting God to humankind through ceremonial practices and sacrifices. However, the new covenant of Christ, which allows you to go to God directly, challenged the authority that religious elites held. For the Romans, having people acknowledge a king above the Roman Emperor caused concern because it could have sparked a rebellion, which had occurred in previous uprisings led by messianic figures. So, in the Gospels during the life of Christ and in the books of Paul after His death, you see all these intersecting dynamics playing out.

Shortly after the ascension of Christ, it became necessary to record the Gospels to maintain the teachings since many in the Church were scattered and persecuted. Moreover, Israelites already had a strong tradition of recording scripture through texts, so the Gospels were a continuation in the same vein. However, like a game of silent whispers, the writings in the Gospel passed down through oral tradition caused some differences to appear in the text. Minor contradictions also occurred due to translation and scribal errors. Moreover, the scribes who wrote them down had their biases about which part of the story they wanted to emphasize. Lastly, there was the development of heretical Gospels like those of the Gnostics, a collective of ancient Christian cults. Many heretical groups promoted ideas fundamentally different from the orthodoxy of mainstream Christianity recognized today.

The Gospels of Matthew, Mark, Luke, and John are considered authoritative. Mark, Matthew, and Luke are called the synoptic Gospels.

The word *synoptic* has etymological roots in two Greek words: "syn," which means together, and "optic," which means seen. So, it is best to study these works as a group due to their similarities and overlaps. The Gospel of John is a more spiritual book and does not fall under the banner of a synoptic Gospel. However, it is also valid. Arguably, because of its more spiritual and esoteric approach, the Gospel of John may have had some gnostic influences from early Christian groups that dealt more with the mysticism of the faith.

By the time the early church took shape, many conflicting Gospels were circulating. So, believers had to develop a way to determine which Gospels were authentic and which should be rejected as heresy. Early Christians used a variety of criteria to determine which Gospels were authoritative and which were not. The date when the Gospel was written was crucial because the closer it was to the life of Christ, the more likely it was accurate. Secondly, the early Christians rejected Gospels written under pseudonyms, which is why gnostic texts like the Gospel of Thomas and the Gospel of Peter were rejected. The synoptic Gospels and the Gospel of John were believed by early Christians to have been written by the authors claimed in the title. However, today, many Christians believe this was not the case and that these texts were also produced under pseudonyms. The last criterion was how widely the books were accepted. If they were used in many of the budding churches of the time, they were given more authority.

Christianity went through various phases. When the Gospels were written, the church was still a loose collective of scattered groups. The apostles and later the church fathers developed some doctrines of Christianity more clearly. Through this process, splits occurred, resulting in the many denominations today. The earliest formal churches were Orthodox and Catholic structures. The denominations that emerged from the Protestant Reformation and later disagreements are younger and were formed due to various disputes or beliefs. However, core teachings unite different groups. The most essential is confessing that Jesus is Lord, that He died for the sins of mankind, and that only through Him can salvation be obtained.

What Is the Central Message of the Gospel

The core message of the Gospel was established in the Old Testament through understanding the Lord's sovereignty. From Genesis to Malachi, the theme of God judging and redeeming nations is consistently repeated. It lays the foundation for a crescendo of ultimate redemption and judgment. The Book of Revelations was foreshadowed in the prophetic writings as the day of the Lord. This final judgment as restoration of God's Kingdom is outlined and will occur in the future. The ultimate redemptive process and covenant are established through Jesus Christ.

What drives God's mercy is love. The Old Testament symbolizes a marriage with the Israelites embracing adultery by worshipping other gods. Their injustice and exploitative treatment of the vulnerable highlight the lack of love, which is why the Lord called their hearts hardened. By accepting Christ, you are given a new heart. So, instead of working to earn the right to be closer to God, the Lord reforms you as you form a fellowship with Him. Therefore, it is not ritual and obeying the law that purifies you in the new covenant but a love for God that reforms your heart.

This is why the teachings of the Messiah are so focused on the doctrine of love. He criticizes the religious order of the day because they were mindlessly caught up in the details of the law but forgot its purpose. Moreover, much of Jesus's teachings are focused on the poor and vulnerable. The only time in the New Testament where you see Jesus violently losing His temper was in the temple when money changers and merchants were scamming people. You know they were not being honest in their dealings because Jesus accused them of being thieves.

Another core message of Jesus's teachings is mercy and forgiveness. In addition to dying for the forgiveness of sins, Jesus practiced the principles of grace and mercy before His death and resurrection. The popular story of the adulterous woman the village wanted to stone is the perfect indicator of mercy. Although the law commanded that she should be stoned, Jesus facilitated forgiveness by asking that the first person to throw a stone should be sinless. This is to emphasize that they, too, are not perfect and require mercy. Jesus came to remove the harshness from people's hearts and encouraged those who heard His message to find their humanity.

Jesus taught a radical love that is unmatched. Luke 23:34 highlights the remarkable love of Christ when the Messiah says, "Father, forgive them, for they do not know what they are doing." In the middle of being crucified and experiencing the most excruciating pain humanly possible, instead of cursing His persecutors, Jesus finds it in His heart to pray for their forgiveness. Many Christians focus on cleaving to Jesus for their salvation, which is essential, but it is often forgotten that while living, your actions should be driven by love, even to those who do you the most harm.

The fundamental message of Jesus's teachings in His earthly ministry was to start from the center point of loving God and extend that love to humanity. Next to the message of love, and intrinsically linked to it, was caring for the vulnerable. Jesus spent time among sinners and always preached blessings to the poor. When you think of the world today and how many Christians view the homeless, drug addicts, or prostitutes, it seems as if they have forgotten everything Christ stands for.

Who Is Jesus Christ?

The character of Christ changes according to whom you ask. Secular people study the Bible and conclude that Christ was a revolutionary Jewish preacher, but due to the miraculous claims of the Bible, they deny the supernatural aspects of the book. In Islamic tradition, Jesus is respected as a prophet, but claims that He is the Son of God or God in the flesh are rejected. Modern Rabbinic Judaism sees Jesus as one in a long line of charismatic, apocalyptic teachings that arose when Israelites lived under Roman rule. Through the Biblical lens, Jesus is the Son of God and God in the flesh who came to redeem the world.

Jesus Christ.

The Christian conceptualization of Isaiah's words that a virgin would give birth and the child would be named Immanuel or "God with us" is that Jesus fulfilled this prophecy. Therefore, Jesus is the Messiah whom the nation of Israel had been waiting for. Many Israelites resisted this message – and still do today because they believe the Messiah would be a military or political leader, but they missed the spiritual aspect of sitting at the head of an eternal kingdom.

In essence, Jesus is the culmination of God's relationship with His people and all the nations of the Old Testament. The cycles of judgment and redemption all lead to the revealing of Christ as the Messiah. When God explains to Job that His ways are not easily understood, a part of the picture is revealed with the incarnation of the Messiah. The suffering, judgment, and subsequent redemption that God continually shows Israel is revealed in a cosmic form going back to Adam and the original sin. Before the kingdom is instituted on earth, God has made a way for His people to spiritually fellowship with Him through the blood of Christ.

Christ is the Word through which all was created. So, the restorative power of salvation comes through Him alone. No other sacrifice would have been worthy, so God had to come in the flesh for the completed work of the Old Testament to be manifested. Instead of focusing on a promised land, God expanded the conception of His kingdom to a spiritual realm so that wherever people find themselves, they can connect to His presence through Christ.

Parallel Reading of the Gospels for Common Themes and Stories to Emerge

The four Gospels of the New Testament were written within the first century after the death of Christ. The Gospel of John is the youngest and the most unique. There are many similarities between the synoptic Gospels, but the Gospel of John stands out. Unlike the other Gospels, where Jesus shies away from declaring His identity outright as God, He makes these declarations publicly in John. Furthermore, John opens with a more cosmological view of Jesus and does not spend much time on His early origins despite the virgin birth being miraculous. Of the four Gospels, John highlights Christ being on equal footing with the Father, emphasizing the eternal existence of the Son.

Mark is also unique among the synoptic Gospels insofar as it does not spend much time on the birth and early origins of Christ. However, there is much more overlap with Mark and the other synoptic Gospels than with John. Mark is the oldest Gospel in the Bible and the shortest, with some considering it a summary of the other Gospels. There is a view that Matthew and Luke were written using Mark as a source text, but this is not widely accepted.

Luke and Matthew have the most crossover. Some assume this may be because they share common authorship, but the most accepted view is that they were probably composed using the same source document called "Q," which has been lost to history. The synoptic Gospels include stories of Jesus casting out demons but are omitted in the Gospel of John. The divinity of Christ is emphasized in the Gospel of John, so it includes the most impressive miracles, like raising people from the dead and turning water into wine. The earthlier focus of the synoptic Gospels consists of the trial and arrest of Jesus, the final Supper, where Holy Communion was first instituted, and Christ praying for the bitter cup to be taken from Him. All four Gospels include Judas's betrayal of Christ.

Activity 1

Create a table or chart comparing and contrasting the four Gospels of Matthew, Mark, Luke, and John. Include their similarities and differences. Highlight which parts of the narrative each Gospel emphasized and summarize the core message carried through in all four texts.

GOSPEL	SIMILARITIES	DIFFERENCES
Matthew		
Mark		

GOSPEL	SIMILARITIES	DIFFERENCES
Luke		
John		

Jesus in Contemporary Life

Jesus, in the Christian view, is the eternal sacrifice and the only gate through which the Father can be accessed. However, some contemporary progressive Christianity rejects the exclusivity of Christ as the way to access fellowship with God. Furthermore, some Universalist doctrines degree that Christ saves everyone, including those who reject Him. However, the faith's mainstream view accepts Christ as the only way to connect with the Father.

Christ preached that it is easier for a camel to pass through the eye of a needle than it is for a rich man to enter the kingdom of heaven (Matthew 19:24). Furthermore, when a rich man asked Him how he could be perfect in addition to following the law, Christ told him to sell his belongings and follow Him, which was too much of a burden for the man to handle (Mark 10:21-22). Considering the materialist outlook and the emphasis on acquiring wealth that permeates the global culture, including the church, some teachings of humility and the irrelevance of earthly treasure must be highlighted.

Social media and online entertainment have created an environment that encourages people to be more self-serving and self-centered. Christ emphasized that you should love others more than yourself. The Messiah did not place a magnifying glass on self-love but took on the most selfless act of sacrificing His life for the world. Even if a person does not accept the Biblical narrative as literal, the symbology of putting yourself before others is striking. The narcissism that is promoted by a self-obsessed culture is far from the example of Christ. If you consider that Christ is God in the flesh and He stepped down from His throne to dwell among humanity, thinking about how humble you are in this light can be transformative. The message of Jesus is eternal, so its application today is as new as when it was revealed two millennia ago.

The modern age is addicted to constant media, which encourages people to covetously compare lives. Some people emerge at the top and are put on a pedestal like the ancient kings who compared themselves to gods. If Jesus encourages people to love God above all and leave everything behind to follow Him, then these actions prove there is a clear misalignment with the scriptures. Jesus states that He will return not as a peacemaker but to judge the world, which begs the question of this modern idolatry and injustice that is storing up God's wrath in this age.

The Bible teaches that you should take the log out of your eye before looking to take the speck out of your brother's eye (Matthew 7: 3-5). When the Gospel is held up as a mirror, how well do you do? Intellectually studying scripture can be rewarding, but the true riches of the Bible are in its practical application. There is no better example than Christ in the narrative because He represents the fulfillment of all laws and prophecy. Therefore, when you measure yourself, Jesus should be the measuring stick. Although you will always fall short, which is why Christ's sacrifice was necessary, the life of a believer is built around striving toward the example of Jesus.

Activity 2

How can the teachings of Jesus to love your neighbor, love your enemies, and love God above all be applied in the modern era? What is meant by love according to the Biblical understanding? When answering this question, consider world events in the news and your personal life.

Section 7: The Book of Acts: The Growth of the Church

The period immediately after the resurrection and ascension of Christ was the liveliest in the church's development. The excitement and concern around this new, budding religion caused many controversies. Furthermore, like with any movement early on, what they believed and practiced was still being developed. The Biblical text Acts of the Apostles covers this vibrant and volatile period in the early church. Acts outline how the church was established under the leadership of Peter and the missionary activities of Paul.

A few main topics are covered in this engaging book, including the function of the Holy Spirit, the persecution of Christians, and the spread of the church to all nations. Where the Old Testament deals mainly with the story of Israel's relationship with God, the Gospels reveal how God is sovereign over all. Therefore, salvation was opened to the Gentile nations through the death and resurrection of Christ. When the views of gods were attached to nations and empires, this revolutionary idea that a God transcends geography, culture, and politics seemed radical. The Book of Acts contextualizes how this new and extreme idea spread and how people embraced this new revolutionary faith.

Authorship and Historical Context of the Book of Acts

The same individual who wrote the Gospel of Luke was responsible for the authorship of the Acts of the Apostles. Some argue it was Luke. Others say the Gospel writer used a pseudonym. Either way, textual analysis links both books to the same author. Acts were written after the Gospel of Luke between 75 AD and 95 AD. Many believe that other than Paul, Luke wrote most of the New Testament.

Although Luke was not an eyewitness to the ministry of Christ, he was a learned man who did extensive research interviewing people who witnessed the events. He traveled with Paul and likely met with many other apostles on his journey. Luke's professional background was as a physician, so he was among the highly educated class of his time. The systematic and detailed way he wrote is why he is regarded as one of the era's greatest historians.

Acts cover a large chunk of the early church's development, spanning over 30 years. The book outlines the 40 days after the resurrection until the ascension of Christ. It highlights Paul's conversion and how the Church's beliefs became solidified early on. The Acts of the Apostles highlight the function of the Holy Spirit, the third person of the Trinity, under most mainstream Christian doctrines. John 14:26 says, "But the Advocate, the Holy Spirit, whom the Father will send in my name, will teach you all things and will remind you of everything I have said to you." In Acts, you find the Holy Spirit moving in numerous ways so the church would be rightly guided in its infancy.

The geographical, political, and social setting of Acts occurs in the Roman Empire. The church spreads from the Near East in Israel into other Mediterranean parts of the Greco-Roman world in metropolitan cities like Corinth, Antioch, and Rome. The book further outlines how the religion spread into North Africa and the other travel routes that turned Christianity into a global faith. Although other missionaries are mentioned, Acts primarily focuses on Peter in the first half and Paul's work in the second half.

Acts highlights the triumphs and tensions within the early faith. It deals with issues like the baptism of Gentiles, whether they needed to keep the same purity law as Jews, and the struggles early Christians had against Jewish and Roman authority. The book ties into the Biblical theme of God's sovereignty embodied in Peter's announcement that believers should follow the commands of God instead of the authority of men.

The Apostles and How They Grew the Catholic Church

It is easy to get swayed by denominational thinking when you approach the word Catholic. The first thing that pops into the mind when considering the word *Catholic* would be the Roman Catholic Church or the practice of Catholicism. However, this is a narrow view of the concept and the history of the church.

The establishment of the Catholic Church is the institution of Catholicism as the creation of a global church.

The linguistic root of "Catholic" comes from the Greek "kata," which means "according to" and "holos," meaning "the whole." A simple way to understand it is that Catholic means "universal." Therefore, the establishment of the Catholic Church is not the institution of Roman Catholicism as it is denominationally understood today but as the creation of a global church. In the earliest days of the faith, there were loose Christian cult groups that studied whatever they could get their hands on and had many diverse beliefs. The establishment of the universal church under the operation of the Holy Spirit outlined in Acts is the story of how the church became unified.

When the church was in its budding stages, there was confusion. Christ had ascended, so the disciples who had followed him for the last few years were left almost without direction. However, before His departure, Jesus instructed them to go out into the world and be witnesses for Him. The beginning of church started in Jerusalem when many priests converted and abandoned temple service to become Disciples of Christ. As people saw their leadership now submitting under the apostles, they also joined, and the church grew exponentially. The church reached Cyprus and Southern Galatia from the starting point of Jerusalem. Next, the church spread to Greece and Ephesus. Eventually, the witnesses reached Caesarea and finally Rome.

According to the Biblical narrative, the Holy Spirit is responsible for the miraculous ability of small Christian cult groups to spread into a world religion. The start of the Holy Spirit's work to spread the faith in the Book of Acts began with Pentecost or the Feast of Weeks, a Jewish celebration 50 days after the Passover. Acts 2:1-3 describes the miraculous events that happened when the apostles were gathered at the celebration. The scripture describes a gush of wind, a thundering sound, and the strange occurrence of tongues of fire resting on them. A miracle occurred because all the men present could understand one another even though they spoke different languages.

This event can be linked to the Old Testament story of the Tower of Babel when the tongues of the nations were confused. The movement of the Holy Spirit now reunited the languages of the nations, not to do the desires of humankind but to promote the kingdom of God. The Holy Spirit resting upon the apostles and giving them the understanding of different languages and for people to hear what they spoke made them effective witnesses to go out into all the nations. There is debate about whether this verse should be interpreted literally or figuratively. Either way, from that point on, the decentralization of the Gospel was solidified, and the God of Israel became the God of the world.

Activity 1

Create a map of how the early church spread from a small corner of Jerusalem to Rome. Plot the key points according to Acts and explain what significant occurrences happened.

From Jerusalem to Rome: How the Faith Conquered the World

Before the ministry, death, resurrection, and ascension of Christ, the scriptures center belief in God around Israel. From the time of Moses, they look toward the promised land. Interestingly, although Moses played a pivotal role in delivering the law, he never entered the land. He led the Hebrews right onto the doorstep of Canaan, but Joshua was chosen to take them in after spending 40 years in the wilderness.

There was a key message the people missed, but Moses understood. It was never about the Promised Land but about dwelling in the presence of the Lord. This is why a journey that was meant to take a few weeks extended into decades. Even in the wilderness, the Israelites' needs were met because they were close to God. When they fell, God made a path of redemption.

In the story of Genesis, the progenitors of humanity were deceived by the serpent, which caused the fall. In the Torah, there is an account where Israel was attacked by serpents, and in order to live, they had to look toward a bronze serpent elevated on a staff. This bronze serpent was a precursor to Christ, who, in the new covenant, humanity had to look toward redemption. Like Christ was reflected in the bronze serpent, so too was the Holy Spirit reflected in the Tower of Babel's account of confusing the tongues of the nations to the Pentecost when the unity of the tongues of the nations was restored to spread the Gospel of Christ.

Therefore, through the Christian paradigm, the sole reason the church could spread from Jerusalem to Rome was because of God's presence or the Holy Spirit being with the apostles and early disciples. The division of nations God caused as a judgment was now restored through the united banner of the church. Under Christ, there was no more Jew or Gentile but one nation.

This declaration that Christianity puts humanity under one united national banner was controversial in the ancient world, especially considering the Roman Empire. Christianity spread fast, so eventually, the masses declared that the true king was Jesus. Roman society was conformist, so acknowledging a king above the Emperor threatened the Empire's stability. Hence, the early Christians faced persecution. Furthermore, the rabbinical Jewish system was under threat because a core teaching of Christianity is that you can access the Father directly.

Therefore, the scholarly and priestly classes were challenged, causing further friction.

These conflicts resulted in many arrests and martyrdom. Rather than hindering the growth of the church, early martyrs helped it to spread. Because people were willing to die for this belief, it created a mystique that enticed many to become followers. Therefore, the persecution of Christians had the opposite effect on Jewish and Roman authorities. This transformation of wickedness into righteous goals is an overarching theme repeated from the Old Testament, such as Jonah's disobedience, which brought pagans to call on the God of Israel.

Activity 2

Reflect on the significance of the apostles encountering the Holy Spirit at Pentecost to spread the Gospel to all the nations. Write about differences in how the early Israelites viewed salvation as national and how the new covenant of Christ opened redemption to all nations, including the Gentiles.

_____
_____
_____
_____
_____
_____
_____
_____
_____
_____
_____
_____
_____
_____
_____
_____

Mapping the Missionary Journeys of Paul

Paul's complete turnaround is one of the most drastic examples of an individual changing their path for God. As Saul, a Pharisee, Paul was on his way to Damascus to arrest and kill Christians. Before becoming Paul, Saul was born in Tarsus to strict religious parents who adhered to the

Mosaic Law. Saul grew up to be a religious leader. He was committed to eradicating every Christian, believing he was acting on the will of God. Paul, blinded by religious conviction, would drag men and women out of their homes, violently throwing them into prison.

Paul.

On the road to Damascus, Saul had a vision of Jesus asking why he was persecuting Him. The light of the Lord blinded Saul, who later went by his Roman name, Paul, so the Gentiles he was delivering the message to would receive him more openly. In his vulnerable state, unable to see, Paul followed Jesus' instructions and continued to Damascus to meet Ananias. At first, Ananias was afraid because he knew of Paul's ruthless reputation. However, being faithful to God, he laid hands on Paul, who told him about his encounter with Christ. After Ananias prayed for Paul, he received the Holy Spirit and was baptized.

Once the primary condemner of Christians, Paul immediately went into the synagogues to proclaim Christ as king. Paul went from a ruthless killer and imprisoner of Christians to one of the most famous believers of all time. As his boldness grew, Paul preached the faith more widely. Paul preached in Damascus, Syria, and his home province of Cilicia. After Barnabas asked for his accompaniment, they went to Antioch.

Paul's main aim was to preach the faith to the Gentile nations, so he spent a lot of time among them. He was arrested in Macedonia after being falsely accused of inciting riots because he had cast demons out of a girl who followed him around chanting about how they were merchants of God, telling people how to get saved. The demon in this slave girl allowed her to have supernatural soothsaying abilities that were profitable for her owners. Therefore, after she lost the gift, their anger propelled them to seek vengeance on Paul, which landed him and Silas in prison. Paul's praise facilitated a miracle in prison when an earthquake swung all the doors open, but none of the prisoners escaped.

The second time Paul was arrested was in Jerusalem. Paul faithfully preached the Gospel wherever he went. However, because he taught the Gospel to Gentiles and told them that they did not have to get circumcised or keep Jewish purification laws, the religious authorities again falsely accused him of telling Jews to abandon their traditions. To prove the religious leaders wrong, he went along with Israelite men to complete purification rituals but was arrested for bringing Gentiles into the temple and taking Jews away from their customs. These accusations were false.

While standing trial in Jerusalem, the religious leaders became excessively violent, which prompted Roman authorities to take Paul to Caesarea. Eventually, Paul went under house arrest in Rome where he wrote the epistles to the various churches. The end of Paul's ministry came when he was martyred in Rome, but his work had by then spread the faith far and wide.

Activity 3

Often, the Old Testament speaks about hardened hearts. Through Christ, the Bible provides a way to receive a heart of flesh to replace a heart of stone. The transformation of Saul to Paul perfectly embodies this exchange. Comment on the differences in Paul's character and mindset after he encountered Christ.

_____
_____
_____
_____
_____
_____
_____
_____
_____
_____
_____
_____
_____
_____
_____
_____
_____

Activity 4

Create a map of Paul's missionary journey, including when he was in prison. Highlight the significant occurrences that helped spread the Christian faith.

_____
_____
_____
_____
_____
_____
_____
_____
_____
_____
_____
_____
_____
_____
_____
_____
_____

The Ancient Church and The Modern Church

Christianity is the most widely practiced religion in the world.
https://www.pexels.com/photo/close-up-shot-of-a-person-reading-a-book-with-rosary-5206844/

Christianity is the most widely practiced religion in the world, although, in some parts of the world, Christians face heavy persecution. However, the faith has become mainstream in many nations. Being a Christian in the ancient world was a death sentence, but people could not hide underground because the scriptures commanded the Gospel to be shared. This meant that many of the earliest followers of what was then called "the Way" were signing their own death warrants. This martyrdom was one reason Christianity spread so fast because once the masses saw that people believed in this idea so strongly that they were willing to die for it, many converts were won over.

Like the modern church, there were disagreements during the infancy of Christianity. The faith began in Jerusalem and was first mainly comprised of Jewish people. However, Paul and Barnabas won over an increasing number of Gentile believers. Arguments circulated about whether it should be required to get circumcised. They concluded that Gentiles did not have to get circumcised or align with Jewish purification laws to become Christian.

The principle that allowed Gentiles to keep some of their customs and Jewish converts to keep practicing their own traditions showed that the Christian faith was meant to be open for all nations to be united under Christ. Evidence of this multicultural foundation is alive today when you see nationalities practicing Christianity unique to their cultural identity. For example, the Ethiopian Orthodox Church has an African way of worshiping in its iconography and the drum rhythms it uses during mass, and the glitz and glamor of many charismatic churches have a modern American feel.

The early church pooled many of its resources together and functioned like a community. It was quite different from modern churches that put money together for activities and to maintain church buildings but did not live communally as early believers did. The early church was a community, whereas churches today form part of a broader community. There was more unity in the early church because the idea of a catholic or universal church was embraced more profoundly. Later developments brought along many schisms and conflicts, leading to the present-day denominations.

Activity 5

Now that you have studied Acts and the spread of the early church, are there any significant differences between the church then and now? If so, what are they?

How do you think the modern church can be reformed to align more with the original church after the Holy Spirit at Pentecost?

_____
_____
_____
_____
_____
_____
_____
_____
_____
_____
_____
_____
_____
_____
_____
_____

What are the similarities between the ancient church and the contemporary church? What are the positives and negatives of those similarities when weighed under the criterion of producing committed believers?

_____
_____
_____
_____
_____
_____
_____
_____
_____
_____
_____
_____
_____
_____
_____
_____

How can the positives be enhanced and the negatives be diminished?

_____

_____

_____

_____

_____

_____

_____

_____

_____

_____

_____

_____

_____

_____

_____

_____

_____

Section 8: Wisdom from the Epistles

Epistle is another name for a letter the apostles wrote to the church for correction, clarification, or encouragement. In the early days of the church, the movement was growing, and so much guidance was needed from the apostles to whom Jesus had entrusted to build His congregation. The growing pains of the church and the convert's multicultural nature created confusion and arguments. Therefore, the apostles had a job to clearly define the message of the Gospel and how to practice the faith correctly. These letters address the difficulties of the early faith, which the modern church experiences today. Therefore, studying these letters can provide deep insight into the practical intricacies of Christianity and reveal how the church was established historically.

The Pauline Epistles

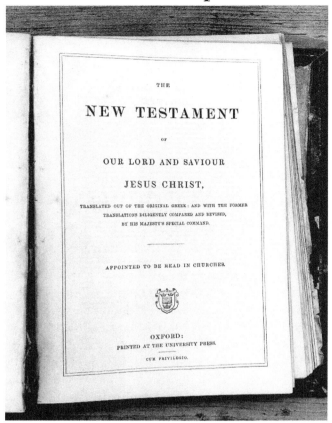

The New Testament includes the Pauline epistles.

As the name suggests, the Pauline epistles are the letters included in the New Testament written by Paul. Some of these books were not authored by the apostle but used him as a pseudonym to give the books more authority. This may seem odd today, but it was a common practice in the Middle East and Mediterranean at the time. The epistles of Paul are divided into four groups: the authentic Pauline, Deutero-Pauline, Pastoral Epistles, and one anonymous sermon some attribute to the apostle. What makes the Pauline epistles unique is that most were addressed to specific regions and people, as opposed to the general or catholic church. These were the letters Paul wrote on his global missions and when he was under house arrest in Rome.

Authentic Pauline Epistles

The first of the authentic Pauline epistles is Romans. The main message the apostle focuses on in this letter to the Roman church is salvation. Paul describes that you are saved through faith in Jesus Christ, meaning you could not earn salvation through good deeds. Paul explains that once you believe in Christ, you will be reformed and exhibit gifts to build up the Christian community. The Roman church was ethnically diverse because it was in the center of the Empire. So, this letter was likely heard by Gentile and Jewish converts in Rome. Considering the diversity within the Roman church, Paul emphasized a unified identity to get the church in the great metropolitan to work together through the unifying force of Christ despite their differences.

Paul heard that the church in Corinth was going down a wayward road, so he composed the first epistle of Corinthians to offer guidance and correction. The apostle was on a missionary trip in Ephesus when he received a letter from the church in Corinth that concerned him. A member named Chloe wrote to Paul, informing him about quarreling in the church and providing other details about what was happening. The letter was written around 55 AD and addressed to the church in the city Paul had founded while there. The congregants had become prideful and justified sexual immorality. Paul provides the most exhaustive Biblical definition of love in this letter in 1 Corinthians 13:4-7. He explains to the church how they acted worldly with their infighting and behavior. Paul describes how the body is a temple and how the church's conduct should reflect their born-again nature. The main message of this letter is that everything the church does should be for the glory of God.

The second book of Corinthians is a continuation of the first epistle Paul wrote to this church. After hearing how the church of Corinth had corroded, the apostle made a journey to the city. After visiting the church, Paul went back to Ephesus and wrote to them again, expressing his sorrow. However, this letter has been lost to the passage of time; 2 Corinthians is a letter Paul wrote while in Macedonia after Titus sent him a report of good news of improvements in the church. This letter was written around 56 AD. In this second epistle, Paul reinforces the idea of unity after many in the Corinthian church repented of their wicked ways. However, some congregants had found Paul's humble nature concerning, so they doubted his authority. Therefore, Paul reinforces his role by emphasizing that he is just as important as the other apostles and gives some details about his life. The apostle highlights that forgiveness and reconciliation are the cornerstones of maintaining the church.

In 51 AD, Paul founded a church in Galatia, which is part of Turkey today. Paul writes to the church in Galatia because numerous false teachers had sprung up claiming that to be Christian, believers must observe the purity laws given to Israel in the Old Testament. Paul's message to this church is that they should focus on the saving grace of Christ through faith in Him instead of falling victim to legalistic false teachers. The mixture of Jews and Gentiles in the church created a theological issue concerning the importance of the Mosaic Law. One group insisted that to be saved, Gentile converts had to be circumcised. Paul rejected these claims in this letter by highlighting that faith in Christ is the only way to redemption.

Paul was incarcerated in a Roman cell while writing Philippians. Conditions today in modern jails are like a five-star hotel compared to ancient prisons. So, you can imagine how much the apostles suffered. Amid this hardship, Paul wrote to the church in Philippians to emphasize joy, which seems counterintuitive. Paul highlighted that there is an abundance of joy in being a disciple of Christ, and regardless of what people go through, the service of the Lord is uplifting. This message is especially profound and inspiring, considering Paul's dire circumstances.

The first book of Thessalonians is the earliest of Paul's letters, dating back to 51 AD. Paul wrote to Thessalonica a few months after establishing the church in the region. When the apostle wrote to the Thessalonian church, he was on a mission in Corinth. Of all of Paul's letters, this one speaks clearly about the end-times events. He highlights the return of Christ and how believers will be united with Him. Paul provides words of encouragement because the Thessalonians remained faithful despite persecution. Paul might have mentioned the return of Christ in this letter to give the church struggling under oppression something to look forward to.

Paul addresses this letter to Philemon, a leader in the Colossians church, instead of addressing the church in general. From the letter, you can tell that Paul and Philemon had a close friendship. Philemon was an early Christian slave owner who hosted a church in his home. One of the more controversial aspects of the Bible, often emphasized by critics, is that there is no outright condemnation of slavery in the New or Old Testaments. However, the practice was common at the time, so it was not frowned upon like it is today. Paul sent Onesimus, a runaway slave, back to Philemon, asking his friend to receive him with grace because he was now a believer. The letter emphasizes that even in a master-slave relationship, love must be shown among believers.

Deutero-Pauline Epistles

The Deutero-Pauline epistles are in line with the ancient tradition of the early church, where pseudonyms were used to give texts higher authority. Although Paul did not author the Deutero-Pauline letters, and some would call them forgeries, they form part of the Biblical canon. The Deutero-Pauline epistles shared common themes with Paul's authentic letters and were likely inspired by them. These letters include Ephesians, Colossians, and 2 Thessalonians. Furthermore, the pastoral epistles of 1 Timothy, 2 Timothy, and Titus are part of this group because the scholarly consensus is that Paul never wrote these books either (Ehrman, 2009). Although these letters were likely not written by the apostle, they may have been composed by his followers, so their teachings are considered valuable, so they are included in the Biblical canon.

Although the modern scholarly consensus is that the Deutero-Pauline letters were not written by Paul, they are constructed in a way that seems like his apostles wrote them. Many believe these letters were written by one of Paul's followers after his death. The Epistle of Ephesians was likely written sometime in the 60s AD. The writing of Ephesians under the pseudonym of Paul again calls for unity in the church, saying believers should be committed to God first and should also be committed to one another. The letter encourages believers to remain steadfast in their faith despite their struggles.

Thessalonians 2 is another letter that may not have been written by Paul but contains the same teachings. This letter speaks to the church's fear that the return of Christ had already occurred. The writer assures the church that Christ has not yet returned and provides signs to look out for to know if it is the second coming. The author writes about a great falling away from the faith that will occur and introduces the concept of the antichrist or, as the letter refers to, "man of sin" and "The son of perdition." People argue whether this refers to a system or an individual. Thessalonians 2 is heavily concerned with the signs of the end times.

Colossians is the last of the Deutero-Pauline epistles that do not fall into the pastoral category. It focuses on the sufficiency of Jesus for redemption and salvation. Some believe Paul wrote this letter from prison, but the scholarly consensus asserts it was likely one of Paul's followers who composed it after his death. The church in Colossae was experiencing a plague of false teachings, including Jewish legalism and mysticism. Therefore, the letter emphasizes that the death, resurrection, and ascension of Christ are central to the faith, and anything else added to that is unnecessary. The author encourages the Colossians to trust in their faith in Christ instead of trying to earn salvation through other means.

Pastoral Epistles

The pastoral epistles address leaders in the early church. They are predominantly concerned with structures, organization, and sound doctrine. These letters instruct how a church should be run, its operations, and what is expected from the members and leadership. The pastoral epistles include the first and second Timothy and Titus. These books form part of the Deutero-Pauline tradition because they use the apostle as a pseudonym. However, many modern scholars have determined that the books were written by followers of Paul and not by him directly. If you consider how communally early church members lived, it is almost as if pastoral epistles are governmental documents rather than constitutions.

According to the opening verses of 1 Timothy, it was written by Paul to Timothy while he was in Macedonia. However, there is evidence in the text that it was produced later. For instance, the linguistic structure of the letter aligns more with second-century writing than the time it claims to be from, so it was likely written pseudonymously. The work has some gnostic elements, putting a lot of emphasis on the ascetic parts of the faith. The letter mentions different positions in the church, including bishop, deacon, and elder. It speaks of widows and how they should be given financial support by the congregants, again emphasizing a collectivist attitude among worshippers. A more controversial part of the letter is the assertion that women should remain silent in church, which has caused modern debate about whether women should take up office.

The second book of Timothy reiterates ideas put forward in the first epistle of Timothy. Again, the leader is encouraged to stand on the true teachings of Christ, shunning anything immoral. The false teachers who reject Christ are compared to individuals who crafted the golden calf in Moses's time. The letter highlights how these idol worshippers died and states that those who reject Christ will meet a similar fate. Although the letter is written under a pseudonym, it is presented as the last words of Paul, who was aware he would soon die under Roman imprisonment. Instead of expressing concern for his situation, he focused on the church, reinforcing the selfless and collectivist attitude believers should embrace.

The letter of Titus is written as if it were the words of Paul, but modern scholars reject the idea that these were the words of the apostle, asserting that it is a work produced after his death. However, the same ideas contained in the undisputed letters are present. In this letter, the author addresses Titus, one of Paul's companions in Crete. The writer emphasizes that although Christians live in a Godless culture, they can resist these temptations and hardships by being reformed by their belief in Christ. Titus was tasked with removing false teachers and replacing them with Godly people to direct the church in the right direction.

Anonymous Sermon

Although some attribute the letter of Hebrews to Paul, the book does not explicitly list the author. The scholarly consensus is that it belongs not to Paul but rather to another unknown author, which is why it is considered an anonymous sermon. One theory is that this was a sermon Paul preached, which was later recorded in this book. The main message of this letter was for Jewish followers of Christ to hold onto the new covenant under the Messiah instead of returning to the Old Testament ways.

Activity 1

Break into groups of three or four. Assign an epistle to each group. Discuss the main message of your chosen epistle and present the information in a creative role-playing scenario by putting yourself in the position of the church community receiving the letter.

Catholic or General Epistles

Most letters in the New Testament were written by Paul or at least pseudonymously claimed to have originated from the apostle. The general epistles are letters written by other church leaders at the time. The general or catholic epistles were usually not addressed to a specific person or group but for distribution among the wider church body. The letters establish orthodoxy of how a church should be run and the principles or structures the body of Christ should embrace. They mirror many of the same messages in the Pauline epistles, showing that a common understanding of the faith emerged early on.

Epistle of James

The letter of James was written shortly before the 49 AD council of church leaders in Jerusalem, which determined the Gospel should be spread to Gentile nations. This letter resembles the wisdom literature of the Old Testament, which focuses on the more practical aspects of Christian living. This connection to the Old Testament makes sense because a large section of James's audience would have been Jewish. The main message of the letter was that faith should permeate every part of a believer's life.

First and Second Epistles of Peter

Peter was one of the most important apostles because Christ personally commissioned him to be the rock on which the Church was built. Peter is considered the first Pope in the Roman Catholic tradition. The epistles of Peter were likely written after the death of Paul. The letters of Peter promoted the idea that Christians scattered throughout the world are the chosen people of God, reinforcing the concept that Christianity is not a nationalist faith like many predating religions. Peter encouraged Christians to remain strong in their struggles, live virtuous lives, and avoid false teachers.

First, Second, and Third Epistles of John

The Epistles of John were written between 85 AD and 100 AD, so they led the church into the second century. Since many Christian cults with contradicting beliefs were forming in this era, John was concerned with establishing orthodoxy among the catholic or general church. John condemned teachers who denied the bodily resurrection of Christ and rejected those like Diotrephes, who denied apostolic authority. John established a Godly order that the church should follow for unity of beliefs and structure.

Epistle of Jude

Jude, who was a church leader in Jerusalem, was likely the half-brother of the Messiah. The letter is not focused on a specific region but addresses all believers. This letter was written between 65 AD and 80 AD. The primary purpose of Jude was to warn Christians about false teachers penetrating the church to promote evil doctrines. Like the other epistles, Jude encourages believers to persevere while refraining from false teachers exhibiting ungodly behaviors, like chasing status, constantly complaining, and following their desires instead of the instructions of God.

Non-Canonical and Lost Epistles

You can tell that some letters written by apostles to the church have been lost. Paul references previous letters in Corinthians, but these epistles have not been found and are not part of the Biblical canon. Some letters dated to around the same time as many of the works in the Bible, but they did not make it into the canon for various reasons. The practice of writing letters of encouragement and correction to the church did not end with the early apostles. The church fathers of the first and second centuries wrote many letters to various churches, which helped shape how Christianity is viewed today and assisted in defining some of the foundational doctrines of the faith.

Activity 2

Using the style and tone of the New Testament epistles, write a letter to a modern church community addressing some of the themes explored in these scriptures.

_____
_____
_____
_____
_____
_____
_____
_____
_____
_____
_____
_____
_____
_____
_____
_____
_____

Activity 3

Create a chart to compare and contrast each apostle's teachings on faith, leadership, and forgiveness. Note the similarities and differences so that you can unveil the different approaches of each apostle.

APOSTLE	SIMILARITIES	DIFFERENCES

Section 9: Understanding the Book of Revelation

The Book of Revelation is the most symbolic and esoteric scripture in the Bible. Although Old Testament prophecies from Isaiah and Ezekiel used the same coded language, the mystery of Revelation has captured the interest and imagination of many worldwide. Humans in various cultures throughout the ages have always been obsessed with the world ending. Many myths and stories have been composed about how the destruction of creation will ultimately come about. The Book of Revelation aligns with this ancient intrigue of humanity meeting its end. Considering the persecution the early church faced and the oppression of the Israelites under Roman rule, it is easy to see why many at this time would want to know about the signs of the end. Revelation paints a descriptive and symbolic picture of what will happen in the last days and what believers can expect and should prepare for.

The Book of Revelation aligns with this ancient intrigue of humanity meeting its end.

History and Literary Structure of Revelation

The Book of Revelation was written after Jerusalem was destroyed by the Romans in 70 AD. Therefore, the Jewish community and Christianity, essentially an apocalyptic sect of Judaism, became a real concern. Revelation was written between 90 AD and 100 AD. Most scholars date it to about 96 AD. The book was written by John the Elder, known as *John of Patmos,* because it was where he got the vision. There is no indication in the scripture that this John is the same person as the apostle John. They were likely two different people because of the time frame. Furthermore, John was a common name.

It is difficult to understand the meaning of Revelation because modern people are so far removed from the cultural context in which it was written. John was writing to a specific audience of believers who were likely able to understand and decode the symbols of the book far better than people today. Many read Revelation by piecing together prophecies of the past to create a bigger picture. However, this exercise is highly speculative. It is best to study the text as a self-contained unit to get the clearest picture of its meanings.

Revelation is written to seven churches in the Roman-controlled region of Asia Minor, known as Turkey today. John received visions on the island of Patmos, off the coast of Turkey. The writer was likely exiled to the island for his work in spreading the message of the Gospel, which the Roman Empire would have seen as disruptive. The text was written in Greek, which was widely spoken among the Christian community.

The church was experiencing a tumultuous period, which John highlighted in the book's opening chapters. Christians in Smyrna and Philadelphia were socially shunned and widely denounced, placing them in danger of death or imprisonment. The church communities in Ephesus, Thyatira, and Pergamum had trouble integrating and assimilating into the pagan cultures surrounding them. For example, they had to question the morality of eating food sacrificed to idols. The last churches John addressed were in Sardis and Laodicea. These congregations were prosperous and thriving. However, the author referred to them as spiritually dead. Their faith had diminished, so the author attempted to revitalize their zeal for the Lord.

Christians in the Roman Empire clashed with the imperial forces because they could not conform to the Empire's requirements. People were allowed to practice religions of their choice in the Roman world.

However, since Rome was a conformist culture, they still had to participate in the Empire's broader practices. The Emperor was worshipped as a god on Earth, and many temples were built to be devoted to him. Although the public was allowed to worship gods of their choosing, they had to partake in the Empire's religious rituals to create a unified identity. Christians were not allowed to because they saw Christ as the true king and followed the Old Testament prescription to worship no other gods other than YHWH, the same reason the Jewish people clashed with the Empire. Jews and Christians refused to bow to the Emperor as God. Therefore, much conflict and persecution occurred due to this tenet of the religion.

For many in the Christian and Jewish world, this felt like the end, as if God's judgment was falling onto them. Therefore, although the symbolism of Revelation can seem scary and violent, a message of hope is embedded in the book, aligning with the scriptural tradition of encouraging people during hard times. It echoed the tradition started in the Old Testament to maintain faith by trusting in God's sovereignty.

Revelation was written when many Christians were killed for their beliefs and practices. Rumors circulated, and propaganda spread that Christians were wicked rebels looking to overthrow the Empire. Therefore, John emphasizes martyrdom in the text not to push believers to die for their faith but to encourage them to persevere regardless of the political persecution.

Revelation ties spirituality, prophecy, religion, and politics together tangibly by using symbolic language. It is easier to grasp a narrative than to follow a list of bland instructions. Although the story structure of Revelation is not linear, it is captivating enough to hold attention. The powerful symbols used to describe the world and the future of Christianity are why Revelation is one of the most studied texts in the Biblical canon. The scripture was composed to get the people of that time to keep pushing forward and look to the future, but the message resonates with so many today who expect many of the prophecies to be fulfilled and see the writings as a reflection of the modern world.

Activity 1

Construct a timeline of the prophetic visions in Revelation. Research and speculate on what these end-times visions could mean and whether these signs are present today.

_____
_____
_____
_____
_____
_____
_____
_____
_____
_____
_____
_____
_____
_____
_____

Symbology and Interpretations

The Book of Revelation's symbols hold the attention of so many. The book does an amazing job of creating an encoded and symbolic world, from terrifying spiritual and political leaders to monsters and feminine personifications. Some speculate that the encoded language was meant to get Christians to understand it while hiding its true meaning from Roman forces that would aim to stop its spread. Controversies exist around how Revelation should be interpreted due to its deep, esoteric writing. Some assume the book can be understood as a description of the then-Roman world. In this understanding of the text, the prophecies refer to events John believed would occur in his lifetime. Others interpret Revelation as occurrences that will happen far into the future.

Revelation is not written in a logically structured way. The text is written almost dream-like, illogically jumping from one vision to the next in a non-linear fashion. The surreal imagery is captivating, but following along in a story format is difficult. Therefore, piecing together Revelation explanations and placing them onto the historical context's blueprint is necessary. In this way, the symbology of the text can be decoded.

An interesting exploration of Revelation's meaning is its use of numbers to communicate various messages. For example, the text mentions seven churches. Biblically, the number seven represents holiness and completion. So, although the writing might have been addressed to seven churches, it could symbolically indicate that John intended it to be written for the entire body of Christ. Seven is repeated as the seven spirits that burned before God's throne and the seven eyes of the Lamb representing Christ. Therefore, Revelation positions itself as a complete representation of prophecy with multiple uses of seven in the text.

Another repeated number is 12, which represents the followers of God. The 12 disciples and the 12 tribes of Israel all paint the picture of being chosen by the Lord. The number is repeated in the text, with 144000 representing God's people that will enter the 12 gates of New Jerusalem. When you divide 144000 by 12, it is equal to 12000, which is a repetition of the number that emphasizes the link to being under God's nation. The number 666 in Revelation is described as the number of the beast that will mislead the world. Some believe this is not the number of prophesied antichrists in the future, but it represents Nero, the Emperor at the time.

It is difficult to map out a timeline of Revelation, so many theologians and scholars develop conflicting narratives. The fluidity of the time in the dreamy, almost nightmarish visions of John creates a wispy feel, making it challenging to grasp a particular thread to follow. The text jumps around confusingly, indicating that John was writing down what he saw instead of creating a solid story structure to follow.

Revelation uses animals and monsters as symbols. Christ is compared to a lamb because of His sacrifice, and the whiteness of the wool represents purity. Satan and the wicked system are depicted as devouring beasts that come to terrorize and destroy. The climax of this imagery is Christ switching from the vulnerable lamb sacrifice to someone who will destroy the wicked powers of the world. It describes a sharp sword coming out of the Messiah's mouth to destroy the nations. This likely indicates that political decrees will be made to free Christians before establishing the Kingdom of God on Earth.

The controversial reference to the "synagogue of Satan" in Revelation has been used throughout history to persecute Jewish people by fueling anti-Semitic tropes. However, the author did not intend to demonize the

Jewish community because many Christians were Jewish converts. It was probably done to highlight Jewish leadership's collaboration with Roman authorities because the budding Christian movement presented a challenge to their power and put some under their rule in danger by attracting unnecessary Roman attention.

Ultimately, Revelation, with all its deep symbology, is a complex comparison between the powers of the world and how believers should conduct themselves. The persecution experienced by Christians at the time could easily have discouraged them, so Revelation provides hope for a brighter future and justice for those who killed and oppressed them. The comparison is best embodied in the contrast of the whore of Babylon representing the evil powers and the daughters of Jerusalem or the bride of Christ representing the believers. The contrast between a faithful bride and a blasphemous, adulterous whore vividly depicts how far Christian conduct ideally is from the wickedness of the nations that oppress them.

Activity 2

Interpret the following symbols in Revelation:

- Whore of Babylon.
- The Beast from the Sea.
- The Beast of the Earth.
- Image of the beast.
- 666.
- Bride of Christ.
- Seven Seals.
- Seven Trumpets.

Early Christian Understanding of the Book

Considering what occurred then, it is unsurprising that a devotee of the scriptures would write an apocalyptic text. Shortly before Revelation was written, Mount Vesuvius had erupted, Jerusalem had fallen, and the Roman authorities persecuted Christians. The end of the world seemed right next door for ancient believers. Apocalyptic literature is not foreign to the Biblical consciousness because Israel had established a long tradition of prophetic writings in the Old Testament and the epistles. Therefore, the writings of John would not have been seen as odd but offered a lifeline to believers in uncertain times.

Although Revelation spoke of the defeat of evil forces, it was never Christians who were the aggressors. John set up a comparison between the violence and aggressiveness of worldly behavior and the peace Christians embody. The instruction to Christians was not to rebel or wage war but to persevere and believe in God, trusting that He will make the burden lighter. It is a logical message to the early church. Christianity is still growing and far from being a major power in the world. The Roman Empire's military strength was unmatched, so encouraging Christians to fight would have been a death sentence. The Romans were surgical at stopping rebellions around the Empire. However, it was against the teachings of the faith to run and hide without proclaiming the truth. Therefore, Revelation is a reminder to be bold as well as an encouragement.

It was discouraging to have endured the pain the early Christians went through. John's visions highlight God's sovereignty so believers can trust that justice will come. Revelation speaks of plagues that will fall onto the nations, exploiting and killing Christians. Traditionally, plagues in the Bible facilitate repentance from evil nations. The nations would not repent, so Revelation explained how they would ultimately be destroyed.

Since the early church had little means to fight back, they had to accept the injustices forced on them daily. Hearing a message that justice would one day come was the hope they needed to live under the oppressive system without abandoning their faith. Revelation was written in a time of war when Jerusalem fell and the Roman Empire was in an expansionist mode. Considering their immense power, criticizing the Empire would not have been a smart choice for anyone. John had to veil his political criticisms so that if anyone found teaching or reading the text, they would not face the force of the Empire. One way to read

Revelation is as prophecies for far into the future. However, early Christians likely understood it as a critique of the government and authorities while remaining hopeful that the wicked system would get what it deserved one day.

Christianity is an evangelical or missionary faith, meaning its doctrines encourage people to spread the message. Martyrdom was common in early Christianity because people openly preached a religion condemned by the authorities. Furthermore, they highlighted a heavenly King above the Emperor, who was meant to be viewed as a God by the Empire's citizens. Therefore, apocalyptic literature like Revelation gave early Christians a reason to keep holding onto their faith despite the clear negative consequences that were a pressing reality in their daily lives.

Themes of the Prophetic Book of Revelation

The first theme of the text is the corruption, opulence, greed, immorality, and wickedness of the ruling class. The personification of these vices and attitudes Revelation uses is the whore of Babylon. Babylon is the perfect description to address a Jewish audience or anyone familiar with the scripture. The evil and idolatry of Babylon were well-known among the audience of first-century Christians because it was a big part of the Israelite narrative concerning their judgment and redemption through Babylonian captivity. The imagery of a whore communicates recklessness and deep immorality. It links to the Old Testament symbology, where Israel was described as adulterous when they departed from God's ways.

Speech is a thematic focal point of Revelation. The image of Jesus returning with a tongue like a sword to destroy the evil nations highlights the power of speaking. John emphasizes the importance of spreading the message of the Gospel by talking about it. He understood that ideas spread through speech, and in the destitute position many Christians found themselves in, the only power they could use was their words. He highlights how Satan's kingdom uses the power of words to spread their propaganda and blasphemy.

Another core theme of Revelation is the anti-materialist views of Christianity. Through the communication of the vision he received, John emphasized the weakened faith of the church in Laodicea was tied to the wealth they obtained through exploitation, making them more accepting of Pagan ways. He reiterated the anti-materialist message by drawing parallels to Babylon and the Roman system obsessed with luxury. John realized that excessive wealth would lead people further from God. Therefore, Revelation encourages Christians to gain spiritual wealth instead of over-valuing worldly riches.

Revelation shows the difference between the messengers of Satan that lead to death and deceive the masses and compares that to the faithful followers or witnesses of Christ, who teach the truth to inherit abundant life. Therefore, as many of the epistles and Gospels emphasize, being aware of false teachers and doctrines that sound pleasing to the ear was essential. Christians should be rooted in their faith in Christ so that they cannot be swayed by the devil.

Revelation asserts that everyone worships something. The worship Revelation points believers to God and Christ, who laid down His life for the redemption of sinners. The other option of worship John put forth was of the beast or the dragon, representing the Roman or worldly system. However, worship of the latter would lead to destruction because deception is all they had to offer.

In the same lane as worship, Revelation often uses the symbology of a throne to show readers what they are submitting to. The throne of the evil authorities was set up to oppress people, which is why Christians should have worshipped the true King in Jesus Christ, who will help them prosper and bring liberation. The message of hope in Revelation is centered on God being above the powers of the world who oppressed the early Christians. Therefore, regardless of how Christians were tempted to deny their faith, the book encouraged them to trust in the One with true power, even above the Roman Emperors.

Activity 3

Choose a passage in Revelation and express the symbology and its meaning artistically. This can be a drawing, poem, song, or other artistic expression.

Section 10: Applying Biblical Principles: Lessons for Modern Life

Now that you've worked through all aspects of the scriptures, including the Mosaic Law, the wisdom literature, prophetic writings, Gospels, and epistles, you are ready to deeply consider how the Bible can be applied to your life. The scripture is not merely meant to be studied. Only one level of understanding emerges from the scholarly analysis of the text. You must apply the principles in a modern context to unfold the deeper layer.

The Biblical text contains timeless wisdom and principles that can enhance your life in multiple ways.

https://www.pexels.com/photo/scriptures-from-a-bible-5247486/

It isn't easy to see how an ancient book can be relevant in a contemporary context. However, the Biblical text contains timeless wisdom and principles that can enhance your life in multiple ways. Furthermore, the Bible can take you from the material context to reveal profound spiritual truths transcending matter and time. To access this spiritual reality, you need to map the historical understanding of the scriptures onto your modern life to reveal the eternal truths.

The Bible is a lot more than just a book for believers. It is the text connecting you to a loving God and a Savior who sacrificed Himself for the forgiveness of your sins. You must walk through the principles of the Bible to comprehend the character of God and the role He plays in your life; then, you will understand why this sacrifice was necessary and the power behind it. This section of the workbook focuses on applying the Bible to bring you closer to God and grasp more profound spiritual mysteries embedded in the text. In this way, the Bible is not a cold and sterile book but transformed into a living scripture that unleashes an abundance of love, peace, and forgiveness in your everyday existence.

Key Biblical Principles and Themes

Although the Bible was written by many authors over the centuries, the miracle of the 66 books is that a consistent narrative managed to emerge. God's relationship with humanity is not as an aggressive tyrant who oppresses the masses but as a loving Father who guides His children through their rebellion, disobedience, and confusion. Hebrews 12:6 says, "The Lord disciplines the one he loves, and he chastens everyone he accepts as his son." This verse encapsulates why the Lord allowed many hardships to fall on his people. A loving parent does not discipline their child to hurt them but so they can learn a lesson, even though they may not understand.

God's wisdom is beyond the ways of humankind. People may never fully understand the motivations and functioning of the Lord in this life or the next. However, the spiritual journey increases your trust that you are complete in the hands of God. The human compulsion to control everything is deeply ingrained into the collective psyche. Understandably, when you feel in control, it creates security and safety. Spiritual practice is opening your tight fists that want to hold onto what is impossible to grab so you can relax into the open palms of letting go in the assurance that God knows what is best.

The revelation of Christ is realizing that of your strength alone, you can do nothing. Submitting to the will of God means following the Biblical principles He revealed an understanding that the love of God and faith in Him leads to abundant prosperity. Putting your life in the hands of God does not mean you sit idly back and do nothing. It is the opposite because it means all your decisions are made by considering what God would want you to do. When you fail to align to Godly principles and stumble, you will commit to turning back to the Lord continuously, living a life of repentance, and demonstrating your faith in Christ through your work.

Love

The Bible says that God is Love. This is a profound statement because it goes beyond saying that God has or possesses love. It describes love as the essence of the Lord. If God is love, then His actions and interactions with humanity must be viewed through this lens. By the extended Biblical narrative through the scriptures, God demonstrates that His love is selfless and unfaltering. When the disciples asked Jesus what the greatest of all the commandments were, the Messiah replied in Mark 12:30-31, "Love the Lord your God with all your heart and with all your soul and with all your mind and with all your strength. The second is this: 'Love your neighbor as yourself.' There is no commandment greater than these." This shows that love is the central component of faith. As God loves unconditionally, humankind created in His image should show the same love to each other.

The heart of humanity has turned to wickedness, meaning it is filled with hate. Hence, it is so easy to envy, bad-mouth, and embrace selfishness. However, through submitting to Christ, your stone heart is turned into a heart of flesh. The more you gear yourself toward loving God, the more your love for your neighbors and enemies will shine through. The key to self-actualization is selflessly loving as the Messiah did when He died on the cross for your sins. Amid torture, Jesus pleas for God's mercy on the perpetrators because, in His divinity, He understood the actions were ill-informed. This is the standard of love a believer should pursue – that even those who plan to harm you should receive nothing but love from you.

This unwavering love is difficult to achieve. Therefore, spiritual transformation takes consistent effort. A good way to understand it is if you take one step toward God, He will take three toward you. When you practice love consistently through your words, thoughts, and deeds, God will multiply this spirit in you. However, when you consciously and continuously slip into selfishness, God will multiply the same spirit in you. The beauty of the Lord is that His arms are always open, and you can turn to Him no matter how far you've fallen.

Forgiveness and Mercy

Humans are not perfect. Since the fall of Adam and Eve in the Garden of Eden, humanity has turned toward a wicked nature. God's relationship with the Israelites in the Old Testament shows that although His righteous judgment must take place, in His infinite mercy, He always made a plan for His people to be redeemed and turn back to Him. This merciful and forgiving nature culminates in the incarnation, death, and resurrection of Christ.

The imagery of a marriage describes God's relationship with humanity. The church is called the Bride of Christ (Ephesians 5: 22-23). Similar symbolism was used for the Israelites in the Old Testament. God highlights how His people are like adulterous brides because they embrace wickedness and idolatry. However, God is faithful, so He always creates a plan for redemption. By sacrificing His son, according to the Christian understanding, God has paid the final price for humankind to find a pathway back to Him, which is why the Bible asserts that no one goes to the Father except through Christ.

As the image of God, humanity should reflect His forgiving nature. The Lord's Prayer says He should forgive us as we forgive those who trespass against us. So, God expects humanity to show mercy to one another. Christ taught this lesson practically when the people wanted to stone the adulterous woman according to the Mosaic law, but Jesus said that whoever has no sin should be the first one to cast a stone (John 8 7-11). Another analogy Christ uses is that before you remove the splinter from your brother's eye, you should remove the log from your own. Essentially, the Bible teaches that you should recognize your imperfections and that you require forgiveness to freely forgive others.

Justice

God is merciful, but He is also just. Therefore, every sin which is committed against Him must be punished. The crucifixion can be understood as a balance between God's mercy and His justice. Imagine you are before God in a court case. The prosecutor reads out all your sins, and your sentence is announced. God, as the judge says, although you are guilty, someone has already paid your fine, so you are free to go. The death of Christ represents the payment of the debt sin creates.

Embodying Biblical justice in your life means you should not focus on vengeance when someone wrongs you but leave a path for forgiveness and mercy. If you weigh yourself on the scale of justice and trace how many people you have wronged and, more importantly, how often you have sinned against God, the mercy He shows by allowing you to breathe is unmatched. As much as God judged the nations, including Israel, in the scriptures, there was always an opportunity for redemption.

The Bible describes that the Lord is slow to anger, so when His wrathful justice eventually appeared, it was after a long time of providing opportunities for people to adjust their actions. Similarly, if you reflect the spirit of God, your anger should not be reckless and uncontrolled. Emotions are human, and you will lose your temper. However, as a faithful believer, you cannot allow your emotions to control you and should always strive to align your conduct with the patient nature of the Lord.

Faithfulness and God's Sovereignty

You may have achieved something great in your life. You look at your achievements and believe it is your hard work that got you there. However, at any second, it could all be taken away in a multitude of ways that are out of your control. Faith is realizing that everything about your life is in God's hands. Increasing your faith means trusting in the Lord.

In the Christian worldview, it is not your deeds that save you but faith in Christ because faith in a sovereign God puts Him as the focus. God has plans to prosper you, so the hardships you experience are for your benefit in this life or eternity. Therefore, your trust in the Lord should remain solid. Faith in Christ is what justifies you before God. Your works will become righteous not because of your effort but because your belief propels you through a transformation of the heart.

Faith is when you rely wholly on God. When the Israelites were in the desert, they wanted to return to Egypt at some point because, at least in captivity, they knew what to expect. However, they did not realize that belief in the unseen and trust in God, who constantly provided, was greater because ahead was the Promised Land. Merely because it is not in front of your eyes does not mean it is not real. Trusting the Lord even in adversity is a central teaching of the Bible. It can be applied in your life when your back is against the wall – and you have no choice but to turn to the Creator. The Lord sometimes puts people in uncomfortable positions so they can turn back to Him.

How These Principles Fit into the Modern World

The selfless love encouraged by the Bible is needed more now than ever. Every doctrine of the world preaches self-love, self-development, and self-image, meaning selfishness has become a core value in society. Social media enhances this as people constantly promote their ideas, compete for attention, and try to outshine the next person. The love of Christ is selfless. The New Testament teaches that you should love your brother more than yourself. This is almost unimaginable in a modern world that considers this boundless love as *self-destructive.*

Applying the principles of the Bible in the contemporary era means catering to God first.
https://pixabay.com/vectors/business-idea-style-concept-goals-1753098/

Applying the principles of the Bible in the contemporary era means catering to God first and letting His love exude from your life. As you place God as the focal point, your will is diminished, and His will takes over. The world preaches to find yourself, but the Bible preaches to deny yourself. As you submit fully to God, your perception will be radically transformed. Instead of solely wondering how your actions and the deeds of others affect you, you will consider those around you and realize they are as worthy of love as you are.

Embracing Biblical principles in the modern world is a revolutionary act. As Jesus condemned many of the Jewish leaders in the Old Testament because they had lost the spirit of the law, unfortunately, many church leaders are on the same path. It makes no sense that a preacher has excessive wealth and sits among celebrities while people in his congregation suffer. Embracing the spirit of God through the Bible's teachings means alienation in many cases, but like the early church, which suffered persecution, an abundance of light and spiritual transformation is a reward for your steadfastness in the faith.

Personalizing the Bible to Your Life

Personal

Humans are social creatures. So, in essence, your personal life comprises relationships, including friendships, family, and romantic bonds. Scriptures teach selfless love, so this is the core value that should permeate your relationships. Love should be the driving force of how you conduct yourself in your relationships. The love God shows you is what you should put out into the world. Being forgiving, patient, slow to anger, selfless, and encouraging should replace mindlessly tearing each other down. The world promotes competition and envy, but Biblically, collaboration is the guide because scripture commands you to love your neighbor as yourself.

Professional

The Wisdom literature teaches the importance of hard work. A lazy person is not likely to earn as much as a hard worker. So, in your professional life, it is advisable to give your all. However, the Wisdom teachings are based on probability. Therefore, working hard is not a guarantee you will get wealth. Doing the best you can but recognizing it is all in God's hands is how you acknowledge the Lord's sovereignty in your professional life.

The central teaching of the scriptures, which is love for God and your fellow man, should come forward in your workplace. This doesn't mean you should be preaching when it is time for work, but at the lunch table, some evangelism could be helpful if you are a believer. Furthermore, spreading love in your conduct with your colleagues is how you build Biblical professional relationships. Back-biting and snakish attitudes are not what Scripture teaches. Remember, the economic system is in the control of the devil, so it is easy to fall into wicked ways at work. Staying focused on God and relying on His guidance lets you manifest His righteousness, mercy, and love in the workplace.

Honest conduct as a professional is essential. The judgment for exploitation in the Bible is harsh. If you have a business or work for someone, remember the Lord does not look kindly on those who take advantage of others. As much as you need to make money to survive in the world, you should not be so focused on luxury and material possessions that it erodes your moral character. Christ taught that it is easier for a wealthy person to go through a needle's eye than it is to get into heaven. This was not a condemnation of wealth but a warning that materialism can easily corrupt you. A Christian should work to live – not live to work – because then your profession becomes an idol.

Societal

Society is built on Darwinian principles of survival of the fittest. The myth of meritocracy has been shattered, and an increasing number of people are becoming disillusioned with the world's system. The Bible calls Satan the god of this age and ruler of the world. That does not mean Satan is equivalent to God. It also does not refer to Satan sharing in God's power as the creator of the universe. However, it highlights the reality that the institutions and structures of the world have fallen into evil, including the media, education, governments, and the economy.

Think of a simple item like your smartphone. Thousands of people were exploited to create that product. The conditions of the mines where people work for the materials are dangerous, and they are underpaid. Many of the factories that assemble and build phones are also exploitative. A similar route of oppression can be traced to almost every product you own. Therefore, the structures of the world are wicked. The Old Testament nations received the most judgment when they mistreated the vulnerable. In the global economic market, the poor are the most vulnerable, and the system falls apart without their exploitation.

Acting as a Christian should societally require you to uplift the vulnerable like the poor, orphans, drug addicts, and exploited of the world. Therefore, your actions and advocacy should be geared toward ensuring those who need love the most are cared for. You cannot single-handedly change society and shift the evil functioning of the world, but it does not mean you should remain stagnant. Jesus said with faith, the size of a mustard seed, you can move mountains (Matthew 17: 20-21), so it is important to remember the transformative power embedded in you as long as you cleave to the will of the Most High.

Activity

Reflect on the themes and principles in the Bible. Highlight some key teachings. Write about how you can apply these principles in the various areas of your life, including family, finance, relationships, and anything else you wish to include. Think about your triumphs and struggles and how you can use Biblical principles to navigate these complexities.

_____
_____
_____
_____
_____
_____
_____
_____
_____
_____
_____
_____
_____
_____
_____
_____
_____
_____

Conclusion

Now that you have worked through this activity book, the Bible has been demystified. You have the foundational knowledge to excel in continually discovering scripture's truth. Not every lesson may have resonated with you now, but as life evolves, you will see some parts of the book become more relevant when you revisit them. Therefore, feel free to work through the exercises as often as needed and review the theoretical explanations as your knowledge deepens.

Studying the Bible is not a once-off activity. The living text reveals new layers the more you explore it. This workbook is like a launching pad off which you can be blasted into new territories. Exploring becomes easier when you know where to look and have a map. However, it is only on the journey that you truly unlock the full capabilities of the adventure. The difference between reading the Bible and living its principles is like looking at a natural wonder on television or in a picture and seeing it in real life. If you saw a photo, you might be able to describe it in detail, but when you are in the middle of a miracle, you experience it and are profoundly transformed.

This book was crafted to tie the scholarly view of the Bible with the practical and spiritual aspects of the text. The difference between knowledge and wisdom is experience. You can read a million books about the details of heart surgery, but you'll never gain the expertise unless you get on the surgery floor and begin operating. The same applies to dissecting the Bible. Some of the most profound lessons are only found by putting the work into practice.

Although you are at the end of this book, you are only starting your journey. People have dedicated their lives to studying and living the scriptures. As you follow the threads woven into these practical activities, your path continues further into new wonders. God is perfect, and as you study the Bible to get closer to God, you will travel the lifelong journey of perfecting yourself through the grace of Christ. This book is a tool to help strengthen your relationship with the Most High and help you follow Biblical principles under the sovereign guidance of the Lord. The Lord's justice, mercy, and grace govern all, so by connecting to His power through the study and application of scripture, you can rest in the loving palms of God.

If you enjoyed this book, a review on Amazon would be greatly appreciated because it would mean a lot to hear from you.

To leave a review:

1. Open your camera app.
2. Point your mobile device at the QR code.
3. The review page will appear in your web browser.

Thanks for your support!

Check out another book in the series

References

Kapp, Tristán. (2020). Towards a promised land: Tracing the origins of Israel and the Colonization of Canaan from Joshua 1-12 to Judges 1-2. 10.13140/RG.2.2.16111.87209.

Let There Be God: How Yahweh became "God Almighty." (2022, June 22). Big Think. https://bigthink.com/the-past/yahweh-god-origins-israel/

Norman, J. (n.d.). The Gezer Calendar, One of the Earliest Surviving Examples of Written Hebrew: History of Information. Historyofinformation.com. https://www.historyofinformation.com/detail.php?id=1280

Smith, M. S. (2004). The Memoirs of God: History, Memory, and the Experience of the Divine in Ancient Israel. Fortress Press.

Smith, M. S., & Miller, P. D. (2002). The Early History of God: Yahweh and the other deities in ancient Israel. William B. Eerdmans Publishing Company.

What Was the Significance of the Commands Against Mixing Different Things in Deuteronomy 22:9–11? (n.d.). GotQuestions.org. https://www.gotquestions.org/commands-against-mixing.html

New International Version. (2011). BibleGateway.com. http://www.biblegateway.com/versions/

qdroach. (2013, March 21). Another Reason to Learn the Bible's Overarching Story. BibleMesh. https://biblemesh.com/blog/another-reason-to-learn-the-bibles-overarching-story/

Isaacs, R. H. (n.d.). A Summary of the Torah. My Jewish Learning. https://www.myjewishlearning.com/article/a-summary-of-the-torah/

Ondich, J. (2022). The Torah. Minnstate.pressbooks.pub. https://minnstate.pressbooks.pub/bible/part/the-torah/

Vaillancourt, I. J. (2022, November 6). 10 Things You Should Know about the Pentateuch. Crossway. https://www.crossway.org/articles/10-things-you-should-know-about-the-pentateuch/

Berger, B. (2019, December 5). Theology Thursday: What Are the Biblical Covenants? GCU. https://www.gcu.edu/blog/theology-ministry/theology-thursday-what-are-biblical-covenants

George, J. (2023, June 22). Literary Structure of the Bible: Old and New Testament Books. Christianity.com. https://www.christianity.com/wiki/bible/literary-structure-of-the-bible-11528149.html

Quick Summary – Bible History. (n.d.). Bible-History.com. https://bible-history.com/old-testament/quicksummary

Schochet, D. (n.d.). The Story of King David in the Bible. Chabad.org. https://www.chabad.org/library/article_cdo/aid/520477/jewish/The-Story-of-King-David-in-the-Bible.htm#Davids

Your Adventist Friend. (2022, April 29). Who Were the Judges of Israel in the Old Testament? AskAnAdventistFriend.com. https://www.askanadventistfriend.com/understanding-the-bible/old-testament/judges-of-israel/

An Introduction to the Book of Proverbs | Bible.org. (n.d.). Bible.org. https://bible.org/article/introduction-book-proverbs

Book of Proverbs – Read, Study Bible Verses Online. (n.d.). Bible Study Tools. https://www.biblestudytools.com/proverbs/

Book of Proverbs Overview – Insight for Living Ministries. (n.d.). Insight.org. https://insight.org/resources/bible/the-wisdom-books/proverbs

Gaiser, F. (n.d.). Summary of Psalms. Enter the Bible. https://enterthebible.org/courses/psalms/lessons/summary-of-psalms

Guide to the Book of Psalms: Key Information and Helpful Resources. (n.d.). BibleProject. https://bibleproject.com/guides/book-of-psalms/

Limburg, J. (n.d.). Theological Themes in Proverbs. Enter the Bible. https://enterthebible.org/courses/proverbs/lessons/theological-themes-in-proverbs

Main Themes of Ecclesiastes | Water on Thirsty Land. (2021, May 19). Water on Thirsty Land. https://www.wateronthirstyland.com/ecclesiastes-bible-book-overview/

Parables in the Old Testament – Bible History. (n.d.). Bible-History.com. https://bible-history.com/old-testament/parables

Summary of the Book of Psalms – Bible Survey. (n.d.). GotQuestions.org. https://www.gotquestions.org/Book-of-Psalms.html

The Parables of the Old Testament. (2019, February 20). Livingwithfaith.org. http://www.livingwithfaith.org/blog/the-parables-of-the-old-testament

What Is the Background of Proverbs? (n.d.). Bibles.net. https://www.bibles.net/book-background/background-of-proverbs/

Baxter, M. (1988). The Formation of the Christian Scriptures. Westminster John Knox Press. Cline, A. (2019, June 25). Three Synoptic Gospels – Compare and Contrast. Learn Religions. https://www.learnreligions.com/synoptic-gospel-problem-248782

Ford, C. (n.d.). Christological Controversies in the Early Church. The Gospel Coalition. https://www.thegospelcoalition.org/essay/christological-controversies-in-the-early-church/

Long, K. (2022, September 8). The Synoptic Gospels Compared to the Gospel of John. Bart D. Ehrman – New Testament Scholar, Speaker, and Consultant. https://www.bartehrman.com/the-synoptic-gospels/

Mackie, T., & Sullivan, A. (2017, May 26). Old Rituals & New Realities: The Day of Atonement and Jesus' Death. BibleProject. https://bibleproject.com/articles/old-rituals-new-realities/

Orr, P. (2023, January 10). What Is Distinct about the Theology of Mark? Crossway. https://www.crossway.org/articles/what-is-distinct-about-the-theology-of-mark/

Parton, C. (2012, November 9). Why Did the Early Christians Reject the "Alternative Gospels"? Exploring the Faith. https://exploringthefaith.com/2012/11/09/alternative-gospels/

BibleStudyTools Staff. (2019, January 23). Paul in the Bible. Bible Study Tools; Salem Web Network. https://www.biblestudytools.com/topical-verses/paul-in-the-bible/

Curtis, D. B. (2008, March 30). From Jerusalem to Rome – Acts 1:6-8: Berean Bible Church. Www.bereanbiblechurch.org. https://www.bereanbiblechurch.org/transcripts/acts/1_6-8.htm

Fairchild, M. (2019, May 6). Discover What the Bible's Book of Acts Is All About. Learn Religions. https://www.learnreligions.com/book-of-acts-701031

Henrich, S. (n.d.). Background of Acts. Enter the Bible. https://enterthebible.org/courses/acts/lessons/background-of-acts

Jakes, M. (2023, March 10). Who Wrote the Book of Acts? Biblestudytools.com. https://www.biblestudytools.com/bible-study/topical-studies/who-wrote-the-book-of-acts.html

Nelson, R. (2019, March 29). Who Was Saint Luke? The Beginner's Guide. OverviewBible. https://overviewbible.com/saint-luke/

Stam, K. (2014). Acts 6:7 – The Growing Word | Christian Library. Christianstudylibrary.org. https://www.christianstudylibrary.org/article/acts-67-%E2%80%93-growing-word

Vickers, B. (2019, September 30). What Are the Tongues of Fire? (Acts 2). Crossway. https://www.crossway.org/articles/what-are-the-tongues-of-fire-acts-2/

What "Catholic" Means. (2018, November 19). Catholic Answers. https://www.catholic.com/tract/what-catholic-means

What is the Day of Pentecost? (n.d.). GotQuestions.org. https://www.gotquestions.org/day-Pentecost.html

What is the Meaning/Definition of the Word Catholic? | GotQuestions.org. (2010, November 13). GotQuestions.org. https://www.gotquestions.org/Catholic-meaning-definition.html

Who was Paul in the Bible? (2009, December 12). GotQuestions.org. https://www.gotquestions.org/life-Paul.html

Why was Paul in Prison? (n.d.). GotQuestions.org. https://www.gotquestions.org/why-was-Paul-in-prison.html

A Quick Guide to the Pauline Epistles | OverviewBible. (2018). OverviewBible. https://overviewbible.com/pauline-epistles/Book of Hebrews | Guide with Key Information and Resources. (n.d.). BibleProject. https://bibleproject.com/guides/book-of-hebrews/

Deutero-Pauline Book. (n.d.). Enter the Bible. https://enterthebible.org/glossary/deutero-pauline-book

Ehrman, B. D. (2009). A Brief Introduction to the New Testament. Oxford University Press, USA.GotQuestions.org. (2006, May 16). Who wrote the Book of Hebrews? Who was the author of Hebrews? | GotQuestions.org. GotQuestions.org. https://www.gotquestions.org/author-Hebrews.html

Guzik, D. (2015, December 7). Enduring Word Bible Commentary 2 Thessalonians Chapter 2. Enduring Word. https://enduringword.com/bible-commentary/2-thessalonians-2/

Hultgren, A. J. (n.d.). Introductory Issues in 1 Timothy. Enter the Bible. https://enterthebible.org/courses/1-timothy/lessons/introductory-issues-in-1-timothy

Jude – Bible Book Chapters and Summary – New International Version. (n.d.). Www.christianity.com. https://www.christianity.com/bible/niv/jude/

Just, F. (n.d.). Deutero-Pauline Letters. Catholic-Resources.org. https://catholic-resources.org/Bible/Paul-Disputed.htm

Just, F. (n.d.). Epistles of Peter. Catholic-Resources.org. https://catholic-resources.org/Bible/Epistles-Peter.htm

O'Neal, S. (2018, July 22). Examination of the Pauline Epistles. Learn Religions. https://www.learnreligions.com/overview-the-epistles-of-the-new-testament-363407

Summary of the Book of 1 Corinthians – Bible Survey. (n.d.). GotQuestions.org. https://www.gotquestions.org/Book-of-1-Corinthians.html

Summary of the Book of 2 Timothy – Bible Survey. (n.d.). GotQuestions.org. https://www.gotquestions.org/Book-of-2-Timothy.html

Summary of the Book of Ephesians – Bible Survey. (n.d.). GotQuestions.org. https://www.gotquestions.org/Book-of-Ephesians.html

Summary of the Book of Galatians – Bible Survey. (n.d.). GotQuestions.org. https://www.gotquestions.org/Book-of-Galatians.html

Swindoll, C. (n.d.). Book of First Thessalonians Overview – Insight for Living Ministries. Insight.org. https://insight.org/resources/bible/the-pauline-epistles/first-thessalonians

Swindoll, C. (n.d.). Book of James Overview – Insight for Living Ministries. Insight.org. https://insight.org/resources/bible/the-general-epistles/james

Swindoll, C. (2020). Book of Second Corinthians Overview – Insight for Living Ministries. Insight.org. https://insight.org/resources/bible/the-pauline-epistles/second-corinthians

Theology of Work. (n.d.). Summary & Conclusion to Romans. Theology of Work. https://www.theologyofwork.org/new-testament/romans-and-work/conclusions-romans/

Theology of Work. (n.d.). The Pastoral Epistles and Work. Theology of Work. https://www.theologyofwork.org/new-testament/pastoral-epistles/

What are the General Epistles? (n.d.). GotQuestions.org. https://www.gotquestions.org/general-epistles.html

Whittaker, J. (2022, August 2). Summary of Colossians: Understanding the Basics of Colossians in the Bible. Renew.org. https://renew.org/summary-of-colossians-understanding-the-basics-of-colossians-in-the-bible/

Who was Philemon in the Bible? (n.d.). GotQuestions.org. https://www.gotquestions.org/Philemon-in-the-Bible.html

Koester, C. R. (n.d.). Summary of Revelation. Enter the Bible. https://enterthebible.org/courses/revelation/lessons/summary-of-revelation

Pagels, E. (2012, March 7). Book Of Revelation: "Visions, Prophecy, And Politics." Npr.org. https://www.npr.org/2012/03/07/148125942/the-book-of-revelation-visions-prophecy-politics

Revelation: It's No Mystery. (n.d.). GCI Archive. https://archive.gci.org/articles/revelation-its-no-mystery/

White, L. M. (n.d.). Book Of Revelation | Apocalypse! FRONTLINE | PBS. Www.pbs.org. https://www.pbs.org/wgbh/pages/frontline/shows/apocalypse/revelation/white.html

Are we supposed to let go and let God? (n.d.). GotQuestions.org. https://www.gotquestions.org/let-go-and-let-God.html

Grace Theological Seminary. (2022, May 27). What does faith mean? Grace Theological Seminary. https://seminary.grace.edu/what-does-faith-mean/

Hanegraaff, H. (2023, May 2). Why is Satan called "the god of this age"? Christian Research Institute. https://www.equip.org/bible_answers/why-is-satan-called-the-god-of-this-age/

Love in the Bible | Resource Guide | BibleProjectTM. (n.d.). BibleProject. https://bibleproject.com/guides/love-in-the-bible/

Theology of Work. (n.d.). 10 Key Points About Work in the Bible Every Christian Should Know. Theology of Work. https://www.theologyofwork.org/resources/what-does-the-bible-say-about-work/

Printed in Great Britain
by Amazon

46627062R00079